Selected Poems of
Rubén Darío

Selected Poems
of Rubén Darío

A Bilingual Anthology

Edited, translated, and with an introduction by
Alberto Acereda and Will Derusha

Lewisburg: Bucknell University Press
London: Associated University Presses

Associated University Presses
440 Forsgate Drive
Cranbury, NJ 08512

Associated University Presses
16 Barter Street
London WC1A 2AH, England

Associated University Presses
P.O. Box 338, Port Credit
Mississauga, Ontario
Canada L5G 4L8

The paper used in this publication meets the requirements of the American National Standard for Permanence of Paper for Printed Library Materials Z39.48-1984.

Library of Congress Cataloging-in-Publication Data

Darío, Rubén, 1867–1916.
[Poems. Spanish & English. Selections]
    Selected poems of Rubén Darío : a bilingual anthology / edited, translated, and with an introduction by Alberto Acereda and Will Derusha.
        p.   cm.
    Includes bibliographical references.
    ISBN 0-8387-5461-9 (alk. paper)
    1. Darío, Rubén, 1867–1916—Translations into English. I. Acereda, Alberto, 1965– II. Derusha, Will, 1949– III. Title.

PQ7519.D3 A225 2001
861'.5—dc21
                                                                                        2001018450

Contents

8   *Contents*

Selected Poems of
Rubén Darío

Part I:
Introduction

1

The Poetic World
of Rubén Darío

Félix Rubén García Sarmiento of Nicaragua—better known as "Rubén Darío" (1867–1916)—remains one of the greatest voices in all the lyrical poetry ever written in Spanish. The tone, the exact word, the attention to language on every level, and the resonance of his poetry furnish proof of this assertion. Darío is much more than a singer of princesses, marquises, and swans—symbols, moreover, that are often misinterpreted. He is in fact a poet of wide and varied interests, from the erotic to the religious, from the social to the metapoetic, from the occult to the existential. Everything in Darío is poetry: the beauty and concision of his word, together with the vision expressed in his verse, make it easy to grasp Darío's enormous importance both as a poet and as a man. In tracing the outlines of Rubén Darío's poetry, it should be stressed that any attempt at a schematization or summary of his lyrical poetry may be misleading. For this reason we offer only a note or two on Darío's poetry books and on some of the poems chosen for this anthology. We have intentionally avoided the debate over the concept of *modernismo*. So much has been written from so many viewpoints that any serious treatment would require a separate introduction in and of itself. It is important, however, to stress that when Spanish American poets of the latter part of the nineteenth century turned their attention to Parnassian poetry, and still later to French symbolist poetry, they were in search of new forms of expression and meaning. Thus so-called "modernismo" was born, a fundamentally poetic movement, primarily formal in nature—with obvious sociological implications—that originated in Spanish America and was brought to Spain by Rubén Darío. Such a view does not exclude, of course, the existence of *modernismo* in prose (whether essay, short story, chronicle, novel, or even prose poem), yet the greatest literary achievements of the movement undoubtedly take place in poetry, and more specifically in Rubén Darío, in whose verse *modernismo* reaches its zenith. Without him, literary *modernismo* would not have fully come into being, and with his death in 1916, *modernismo* too would die. It is highly important to differentiate Spanish American *modernismo* from all other forms of so-called "modernist" literature with which the reader may be acquainted: the *modernismo brasileiro* from Brazil, for example, or the *modernisme català* from Catalonia, or Anglo-American Modernism, to name the most obvious. In the same way, Spanish American *posmodernismo*, which refers to *modernista* literature in its final stages, must not be confused with what has come to be known as "postmodernism" in literary theory and Anglo-American studies. For the sake of clarity, then, by Hispanic *modernismo* we mean the literary movement that began in Spanish America around 1880 and lasted into the second decade of the twentieth century. The debate over the concept of *modernismo*, for those interested, may be found in any number of basic studies on the subject. Here we will mention several classic contributions to the field which remain revelant even today: Díaz-Plaja (1951), J. R. Jiménez (1953), Henríquez Ureña (1954), Gullón (1964), Davidson (1966), Schulman (1966, 1969, 1987), Rama (1970, 1985), Anderson (1970), Castillo (1974), Litvak (1975), Perús (1976), Yurkevich (1976), Jitrik (1978), Gutiérrez Girardot (1983), J. O. Jiménez (1985), and Carnero (1987).[1] Since the publication of these standard works, a number of new studies have appeared, the most noteworthy being Azam (1989), Zavala (1992), Cardwell and McGuirk (1993), Montaldo (1995), and Jrade (1998).[2] For an instructive view of the debate over *modernismo* in its own time—that is, at the turn of the century—Zuleta (1988) and Celma Valero (1989) are highly recommended.[3] We hope that readers will arrive at a more objective idea of *modernismo* as they evaluate our assertions in the light of Darío's actual texts. Let it be clear from the outset that the appeal of this anthology does not depend on what may be said here by way of an introductory summary, but rather on our endeavor to restore the purity of Darío's text free from typographical errors and faithful to the first edition of his books, as explained below in the section devoted to "Editorial Criteria"; at the same time, this anthology constitutes one of the very few attempts to translate Darío's poetry into English. As important, prolific, and famous as Rubén Darío is, little effort has been made to translate his works. Back in 1965, the University of Texas Press published an anthology of Darío's poems translated by Lysander Kemp, and so far that translation, long out of print, remains the one source for anyone in need of a selection of Darío's poetry in English.[4] However talented the editor and translator might be,

Kemp's anthology is questionable from a textual standpoint, as are all the studies that utilize Kemp's translations. Other studies that lay out translations of Darío's poems in paragraph form—thereby vitiating the poetic structure so essential to *modernismo* in general and to Darío in particular—are even farther from the original. We now focus on Darío's poetry, giving an overview of the books published in his lifetime. A brief summary of that life, as well as a complete bibliography of his works, can be found at the end of this introduction.

EARLY BOOKS OF POETRY

Poetry surfaced early in the life of Rubén Darío with the production of student works, correct in technique and generally praised. He came to be regarded as something of a child poet, even drawing the attention of the Nicaraguan government. By 1885, the teenaged Darío had already collected a number of compositions in a book originally titled *Epístolas y poemas* [*Epistles and Poems*]; due to editorial circumstances the book would not appear until 1888, and then under a different title: *Primeras notas* [*First Notes*]. This is a book of youth, at times mawkish and overly rhetorical in comparison to later books, the work of a poet just starting out. In 1886, he wrote a series of short poems published the following year under the title *Abrojos* [*Thistles*], a book improvised from anecdotes and reflections of the poet while in Chile. The poem beginning *"Puso el poeta en sus versos . . . "* ["The poet put in his verses . . . "] is a premonition of the pain of a man who, in his profession as poet, suffers the economic misery of the needy—circumstances which Darío himself was soon to suffer. Other poems from *Abrojos*, such as the one that opens with *"Cuando la vio pasar el pobre mozo . . ."* ["When the poor guy saw her pass . . ."], are likewise fraught with biographical elements: these lines briefly refer to Darío's love for a woman from the high society of the Chilean capital, after he happened to see her in the company of another man. In Valparaíso in 1887, the same year that saw the publication of *Abrojos*, Darío took part in the *Certamen Varela*, a poetry competition planned and financed by Chilean politician Federico Varela. Darío won a prize for his *Canto épico a las glorias de Chile* [*Epic Song to the Glories of Chile*] and received an honorable mention for the group of compositions entitled *Rimas* [*Rhymes*] in imitation of Gustavo Adolfo Bécquer, the great Spanish Romantic poet. The *Canto épico a las glorias de Chile* is a patriotic ode, a rhetorical exercise well-crafted but narrowly pegged to the 1879 war between Chile and Peru, the latter being allied with Bolivia; here Darío extols the heroism of Chile and its soldiers in that Pacific War. The book *Rimas*, on the other hand, has many similarities to the poems in *Abrojos*, revealing as well the adoration of Bécquer then current in Spanish America. The poems "*Amada, la noche llega . . .* " ["My love, the night has come . . . "] and "*El ave azul del sueño . . .* " ["The dream's blue bird . . . "], both found in this anthology, serve as good examples of such poetry. Apparently, Darío wrote these compositions in July 1887, in time for the competition in August of that year.

Azul . . .

Darío was never a mere imitator of anyone, as he himself would write years later in the preface to *Prosas profanas* [*Profane Prose*]. And so we find that the real Rubén Darío—and his completely personal poetic voice—emerged in Valparaíso in 1888 with the publication of his first truly great book, *Azul . . .* [*Blue . . .*]. Without question, *Azul . . .* brought about a revolution in the poetry and prose written in Spanish, and thus its importance to literary history, as writer and critic Juan Valera observed even back then. The number of poems included in *Azul . . .* passed through several alterations from the first edition in 1888 through the third edition in 1905, which Darío considered definitive. Thematically, *Azul . . .* sings of love, of woman, of eroticism blended with the pagan motif ("*Estival*" or "In Summer"), of force and of natural love (also in "*Estival*"), and likewise of impossible love ("Venus"). Such poems from the section *El año lírico* [*The Lyrical Year*] breathed new life into the poetry then being written in Spanish. Thus, "*Pimaveral*" ["In Spring"] is a clear invitation to enjoy the season of spring, combined with a mythological eroticism flowing into the sensuality of a refrain that runs from beginning to end:

> *Quiero beber del amor*
> *sólo en tu boca bermeja,*
> *¡oh, amada mía, en el dulce*
> *tiempo de la primavera!*

> [I want to sip at love
> only in your wine-red mouth,
> oh my love, in the sweet
> season of spring.]

"*Estival,*" the second poem from the same section, relates a tragic tale: the instinctive love between two tigers is interrupted by the death of one at human hands, as the intervention of the Prince of Wales cuts short the sensualism of the idyll and the primitive, natural love of the two felines. The solitary tiger's final dream lends the work a tragic tone, making it one of the best poems in his book *Azul.* . . From the section *Sonetos* [*Sonnets*] we have selected "Venus," mentioned above, where we find the poet suffering the realities of unattainable love. Darío speaks to the planet Venus as the goddess of love and symbol of beauty; at the conclusion of the sonnet, her reply becomes a new source of pain, since it is only a gaze of sadness, devoid of hope. In the section *Medallones* [*Medallions*] we find poems addressed to real people who interest Darío either as an expression of heroism or as the idea of the poet as a missionary of art; such is the case here with the poet Walt Whitman. Stylistically, with *Azul* . . . Darío goes beyond the use of traditional stanza forms in a deliberate search for a revolution in poetic structure, utilizing sonnet lines of twelve, fourteen, and even sixteen syllables, rather than the traditional eleven. In a similar vein, the use of alliteration, run-on lines, epithets, metaphors, and a rich association of conceits and wordplay, all point to a painstaking mastery of the musicality of the poem. For these reasons, the book *Azul* . . . must be considered pivotal not only in Rubén Darío's own poetic career, but in the course of modern poetry written in the Spanish language.

Prosas profanas y otros poemas

After *Azul* . . . comes the publication in Buenos Aires of *Prosas profanas y otros poemas* [*Profane Prose and Other Poems*] in 1896, a book later expanded for the second edition in Paris in 1901. Most poems from the first edition were written and published in Buenos Aires between 1893 and 1896, while nearly all the poems added in 1901 were written after 1896. It is important to recognize that *Prosas profanas y otros poemas* represents Darío's poetic eruption, one that continues practically until the end of his life, especially in the next two books. The "*Palabras liminares*" ["Liminary Words"] preceding the poetic compositions in the book comprise the first of only three prologues which Darío would write in the whole *corpus* of his poetry books. In these few pages he denies any intention of writing a manifesto, but does raise important ideas about the aristocracy of thought and the mediocrity of the majority, his loathing of the historical moment in which he had to live, his penchant for the past, his love of the esthetic and the erotic, the question of metrical rhythm, and his Hispanic affiliation, as well as his admiration for French poetry. He also points out his unwillingness to serve anyone as a model, much less to imitate anyone else, all in the name of total freedom, of the artist's need to create. To a large extent the prologue expresses Darío's objective for a book that was to establish a new sensibility in Hispanic poetry. Thematically, *Prosas profanas y otros poemas* is a multifaceted work that includes poems about poetry itself and about poetic freedom, love, the past, paganism, and Christianity. Darío cared very much about the aristocracy of the poet, who is seen almost as a warrior or hero. The swan often symbolizes the originality and personality of the poet or the idea of the poet in solitude, in an inward search for himself ("*Yo persigo una forma . . .* " or "I pursue a form . . . "). The erotic theme is equally fundamental in this book, either by way of an adoration of femininity ("*Era un aire suave . . .* " or "It was a gentle air . . . "), a feminine longing for love and the expression of the human soul ("*Sonatina*"), color as a foundation for love and death, overt sexuality ("*Ite, missa est*"), or simply love and poetry. The subject of the past, already announced in the prologue, finds its embodiment in the eighteenth century as both an aspiration and a presence, or else in the history of Spain. Pagan and Christian elements frequently alternate, whether through mythology and a quest for optimism ("*Coloquio de los centauros*" or "Colloquy of the Centaurs"), or the contrast of flesh and spirit ("*Responso*" or "Prayer for the Dead"). Some of Darío's best known compositions are found in *Prosas profanas y otros poemas*, such as "*Era un aire suave . . .* , " mentioned above, a splendidly erotic song in praise of femininity and the power of the eternal female, now embodied in the figure of the Marquise Eulalia:

> *Es noche de fiesta, y el baile de trajes*
> *ostenta su gloria de triunfos mundanos.*
> *La divina Eulalia, vestida de encajes,*
> *una flor destroza con sus tersas manos.*

> [It is a festive night, and the costume ball
> flaunts its glory of mundane triumphs.
> The divine Eulalia, dressed in lace,
> shreds a flower in her smooth hands.]

The "*Sonatina*" is another poem representative of Darío, one in which—going beyond the apparent petulance of a spoiled girl—he creates an expression for the human soul through the symbolic figure of this heartbroken princess:

> *¡Ay! la pobre princesa de la boca de rosa,*
> *quiere ser golondrina, quiere ser mariposa,*
> *tener alas ligeras, bajo el cielo volar,*
> *ir al sol por la escala luminosa de un rayo,*
> *saludar a los lirios con los versos de Mayo,*
> *o perderse en el viento sobre el trueno del mar.*

> [Alas! The poor princess with the rose-colored mouth
> would rather a swallow or a butterfly be,
> and under the heavens would fly on light wings,
> would rise to the sun on the luminous ladder of beams,
> would greet every lily with the verses of May,
> or be lost in the wind on the boom of the sea.]

Prosas profanas y otros poemas is also the book in which "*Coloquio de los centauros*" appears, possibly one of the greatest poems in the Spanish language, not only for its depth of meaning but also for its perfectly precise form of expression. The "*Coloquio de los centauros*" is an extraordinary harmonizing of the animal, the human, and the divine across the millennia, of life, death, and love, a dialogue between mythological creatures in the Orphic-Pythagorean vein of music and universal harmony. Darío firmly believes in intercommunication in nature, imagines everything as penetrated by soul, and compares divine beauty with that of a woman, revealing a connection to Eastern mysticism and the Cabala of the Spanish Jews. In short, Darío aspires here to the union of all nature, the universal soul of all things:

> *Himnos! Las cosas tienen un ser vital: las cosas*
> *tienen raros aspectos, miradas misteriosas;*
> *toda forma es un gesto, una cifra, un enigma;*
> *en cada átomo existe un incógnito estigma;*
> *cada hoja de cada árbol canta un propio cantar*
> *y hay una alma en cada una de las gotas del mar . . .*

> [Hymns! Things have a vital being: things
> have rare aspects, mysterious gazes;

each form is a gesture, a cipher, an enigma;
in each atom a stigma exists incognito;
every leaf of every tree sings its own song
and there is a soul in each and every drop of the sea . . .]

The heartfelt "*Responso*" dedicated to Paul Verlaine on his death also be-
longs to *Prosas profanas y otros poemas*. The "*Responso*" is no mournful dirge,
but a kind of pagan festival, a glimpse of death in a beautiful form on the
outer edge of Christian consciousness, with hints of reincarnation. At the
end of the poem, the carnal and the spiritual—represented by the figure of
Verlaine himself—are reconciled, and the final triumph of the Satyr unites
the pagan and the Christian elements. Verlaine thus receives divine pardon
and mercy:

Y huya el tropel equino por la montaña vasta;
tu rostro de ultratumba bañe la luna casta
de compasiva y blanca luz;
y el Sátiro contemple sobre un lejano monte,
una cruz que se eleve cubriendo el horizonte
y un resplandor sobre la cruz!

[And may the equine throng flee across the vast mountain;
the chaste moon bathe your face from the hereafter
with white and compassionate light;
and the Satyr contemplate, on a distant mountain,
a cross rising to cover the horizon
and a radiance on the cross!]

The new material included in the second edition (1901) of *Prosas profanas y
otros poemas* consists of a number of poems of real quality, such as the one
that closes the book, "*Yo persigo una forma . . . ,*" in which the poet searches
for the revelation of his own poetic art as a path to self-enlightenment.
Stylistically, *Prosas profanas y otros poemas* contains numerous examples of
freedom in the creation of stanza forms. On the acoustic level the book
establishes the use of free verse, thus pioneering an important verse form
that has become so prevalent in twentieth-century Hispanic poetry. In his
further search for musicality, Darío also turns to hendecasyllables, especially
in the *serventesio* stanza, as well as to fourteen-syllable *alejandrinos*. More-
over, *Prosas profanas y otros poemas* includes compositions in *romance* form

with dodecasyllables and *alejandrinos*; sonnets with verses of six, eight, eleven, and fourteen syllables; eleven-syllable quatrains, *serventesios* of the Galician *gaita*, as well as *cuartetos-serventesios* composed of twelve-syllable verses; single-rhyming tercets; and a wondrous variety of stanzas which Darío skillfully combines with age-old Castilian meters. For all these reasons, then, *Prosas profanas y otros poemas* goes even further than *Azul . . .* in the renovation of Spanish-language poetry and prepares the way for *Cantos de vida y esperanza. Los cisnes y otros poemas* [*Songs of Life and Hope. The Swans and Other Poems*], the literary highpoint of Darío's poetic career.

Cantos de vida y esperanza. Los cisnes y otros poemas

In the final years of the nineteenth century and the first years of the twentieth, Rubén Darío reached artistic maturity, and it was then that he poured all his knowledge and craft into creating some of his finest compositions. The actual gestation of individual works was almost always hurried, with little care given to sorting and preserving the compositions. In fact, it would be the young Spanish poet Juan Ramón Jiménez who took charge of the poems that, in 1905, became *Cantos de vida y esperanza. Los cisnes y otros poemas*, which stands among the true poetic landmarks written in Spanish. Published by the *Journal of Libraries, Archives, and Museums* in Madrid, *Cantos de vida y esperanza. Los cisnes y otros poemas* brings together compositions written in different places between 1892 and 1905, preceded by a brief but quite interesting "*Prefacio*" ["Preface"].

In the poems themselves we again find a fascinating thematic variety. The theme of poetry and the poet reappears with greatest force in works such as "*Torres de Dios! . . .*" ["Towers of God! . . ."] and the famous poem with which the book opens, "*Yo soy aquel . . .*" ["I am the one . . ."]. The latter is a portrait of his inner life in which Rubén Darío seeks the complete reconciliation of opposites, aspires to universal harmony, and gives a very personal confession of his secret self:

> , *La torre de marfil tentó mi anhelo;*
> *quise encerrarme dentro de mí mismo,*
> *y tuve hambre de espacio y sed de cielo*
> *desde las sombras de mi propio abismo.*
>
> .   .   .   .
>
> *Mi intelecto libré de pensar bajo,*
> *bañó el agua castalia el alma mía,*

peregrinó mi corazón y trajo
de la sagrada selva la armonía.

[The ivory tower tempted my desires;
I tried to lock myself within me,
and got hungry for space and thirsty for sky
from the shadows of my own abyss.

.   .   .   .

I freed my intellect from base thinking,
the waters of Castalia bathed my soul,
my heart made a pilgrimage and brought
harmony from the sacred wood.]

In other compositions we discover the theme of Hispanic cultural solidarity, where life is identified with the Hispanic Union and death with mere survival in a world—the Anglo-Saxon world, and particularly that of the United States of America contemptuous of all things Hispanic. Along this line are found poems collected here, such as "*A Roosevelt*" ["To Roosevelt"] and the first poem from the section "*Los cisnes*" ["The Swans"], which begins "*Qué signo haces . . . ?*" ["What sign do you give . . . ?"] and reveals Darío's anguish at the possible destruction of the Hispanic world at the hands of Anglo-Saxons. Some of the most beautiful verses in the book emerge from the poet's disenchantment:

Brumas septentrionales nos llenan de tristezas,
se mueren nuestras rosas, se agotan nuestras palmas,
casi no hay ilusiones para nuestras cabezas,
y somos los mendigos de nuestras pobres almas.

[Septentrional mists fill us with sorrows,
our roses are killed off, our palm trees used up,
there is scarecely a dream for our heads,
and we are beggars of our poor souls.]

The existential theme is central to an understanding of *Cantos de vida y esperanza. Los cisnes y otros poemas,* either in its life-affirming optimism or its disillusionment in the face of death, with the poet's ensuing anguish. The section "*Otros poemas*" ["Other Poems"] contains the first of the book's nocturnes underscoring the apprehension found in almost all of Darío's poetry. The anguish here is, undeniably, existential anguish—long before that term was coined—since the poet is fully conscious of the inescapable passage of time. Darío molds his personal history with this very anguish, the awareness that life moves ineluctibly toward an end, life viewed as a nightmare from which only death will awaken us:

> *la conciencia espantable de nuestro humano cieno*
> *y el horror de sentirse pasajero, el horror*
> *de ir a tientas, en intermitentes espantos,*
> *hacia lo inevitable desconocido y la*
> *pesadilla brutal de este dormir de llantos*
> *de la cual no hay más que Ella que nos despertará!*

> [the fearsome awareness of our human slime,
> and the horror of feeling short-lived, the horror
> of groping along, in intermittent dread,
> toward the inevitable unknown and the
> brutal nightmare of this weeping sleep
> from which there is only She to awaken us.]

This despairing conception of life—life almost like a poison—is repeated in another poem from the same section, "*A Phocás el campesino*" ["To Phocas the Peasant"], written to his son Rubén Darío Sánchez, a newborn who would die a few months later. Here the poet's disillusionment with life is such that he begs forgiveness from his son for his role in the infant's birth. Personal tragedies, such as the death of two of his children, along with bouts of depression and a hyperaesthetic temperament, would move him to write "*Lo fatal*" ["What Gets You"], the poem with which the book concludes so impressively. "*Lo fatal*" is one of the highpoints of poetry written in Spanish, and perhaps the best of all Rubén Darío's works. Here the poet visualizes human beings as creatures punished precisely for being the most aware of who and what they are. In just thirteen verses Darío manages to sum up the whole existential problem: life and death, anguish and pain, anticipating Heidegger's identification of human beings with their existence, as well as the anguish that reveals the concept of *being* as the flip side of nothingness. Darío's being is changeable: it flows into time, and here may also be found a trace of Nietzsche's nihilism:

Dichoso el árbol que es apenas sensitivo,
y más la piedra dura porque ésa ya no siente,
pues no hay dolor más grande que el dolor de ser vivo,
ni mayor pesadumbre que la vida consciente.

Ser, y no saber nada, y ser sin rumbo cierto,
y el temor de haber sido y un futuro terror . . .
Y el espanto seguro de estar mañana muerto,
y sufrir por la vida y por la sombra y por

lo que no conocemos y apenas sospechamos,
y la carne que tienta con sus frescos racimos,
y la tumba que aguarda con sus fúnebres ramos,
y no saber a dónde vamos,
ni de dónde venimos . . . !

[How fortunate the tree that is scarcely aware,
and more so the hard stone because it no longer feels,
since there is no greater pain than the pain of living,
nor deeper sorrow than conscious life.

Being, and knowing nothing, and being without a true course,
and the fear of having been, and a future terror . . .
And the certain dread of being dead tomorrow,
and suffering because of life, and because of shadow, and because of

what we don't know and scarcely suspect,
and the flesh that tempts with its fresh-picked bunches,
and the tomb that awaits with its funeral bouquets,
and not knowing where we are going,
nor from where we have come . . . !]

Another important theme here, as in other books by Darío, is Christian-pagan dualism, seen in such poems as "*Spes*," "*La dulzura del ángelus*" ["The sweetness of the Angelus"], and "*Divina Psiquis, dulce Mariposa invisible . . .*" ["Divine Psyche, sweet invisible Butterfly . . ."]. Nor is the erotic theme lacking in this book, as becomes obvious in such poems as "*Carne, celeste carne de la mujer! Arcilla . . .*" ["Flesh, a woman's heavenly flesh! Clay . . ."].

In terms of form, *Cantos de vida y esperanza. Los cisnes y otros poemas* is a book written in a state of grace, since its poems—almost without exception—show as much prodigious care in the quality of the acoustical dimension as in the grammatical and lexical.

El canto errante

At times economic hardship forced Darío to write and publish in an effort to obtain some relief. Such is the case, in part, of *El canto errante* [*The Roving Song*], published in Madrid in 1907 with the hope of generating sorely needed funds. Darío himself scraped together enough poems to compose a book by taking a number of compositions written between 1905 and 1907 and incorporating them with many others published earlier in Spain and Spanish America, as well as unpublished poems from previous years. As the title indicates, *El canto errante* refers to the poet roving through a world that is not overly concerned with art and poetry. The fact that *El canto errante* combines older poems with those of more recent composition does not diminish the book's poetic value. It should be understood that *El canto errante* is another work written when Darío stood at the peak of his poetic powers. Here we find several poems of tremendous quality and a range of themes that have now become constants in Darío's poetic output. *El canto errante* begins with a prologue, "*Dilucidaciones*" ["Elucidations"], an assortment of notes and sketches published somewhat earlier in the Madrid press. In a sense, the "*Dilucidaciones*" served as an act of self-defense against attacks by Darío's critics, especially in Spain. The prose here is excellent, and some observations still retain the freshness of the times. For example, Darío writes:

> *La poesía existirá mientras exista el problema de la vida y de la muerte. El don de arte es un don superior que permite entrar en lo desconocido de antes y en lo ignorado de después, en el ambiente del ensueño o de la meditación. Hay una música ideal como hay una música verbal. No hay escuelas; hay poetas. El verdadero artista comprende todas las maneras y halla la belleza bajo todas las formas. Toda la gloria y toda la eternidad están en nuestra conciencia.*

[Poetry will exist as long as the problem of life and death exists. The gift of art is a superior gift that gains entrance to what was unknown before and unsuspected thereafter, in an ambience of fantasy or meditation. There is a music of ideas as well as a music of words. There are no schools; there are poets. The true artist comprehends all styles and finds beauty under all forms. All glory and all eternity are within our awareness.]

In terms of its lyric, *El canto errante* contains some poems—like "*Metempsícosis*" ["Metempsychosis"], written in 1893—that reveal Darío's fascination with reincarnation; in this case, the reincarnated soul of a soldier tells his migratory history. Other poems—such as "*Sum . . .*" and "*Eheu!*"—arise from Darío's concern for the existential situation of human beings, a concern that leads him to create deeply tragic poetry. This sort of composition, evident at every stage of Darío's poetry, shows his least-studied facet: a long-standing interest in esoteric doctrines, quite different from the usual stereotype of Darío as a colorist poet of princesses and swans. No view could be more erroneous. Thus, for instance, Darío writes in "*Eheu!*":

> *El conocerme a mí mismo*
> *ya me va costando*
> *muchos momentos de abismo*
> *y el cómo y el cuándo . . .*
>
> *Y esta claridad latina,*
> *¿de qué me sirvió*
> *a la entrada de la mina*
> *del yo y el no yo . . . ?*
>
> [Knowing myself
> has already begun to cost me
> many abysmal moments
> and the how and the when . . .
>
> And this Latin clarity,
> what good did it do me
> at the entrance to the mine
> of self and no self . . . ?]

Topical verse appears in *El canto errante* as well, and some poems of friendship like those dedicated to Antonio Machado and Ramón del Valle-Inclán. Nevertheless, even in these works Darío's creative talent may be clearly observed. The tone is thoughtful rather than prosaic, and often ironically tragic.

THE LAST BOOKS OF POETRY

Three years later in 1910, also in Madrid, Darío published his next-to-last book of poetry, *Poema del otoño y otros poemas* [*The Autumn Poem and Other Poems*]. Except for the final composition in the book, which dates from 1892, all the poems were written after 1907. Some revolve thematically around love or the Hispanic race, and others were composed for special occasions, or to memorialize friendships. A truly outstanding work opens the book, the "*Poema del otoño*," another major poem in the Darío canon. This is one of his most optimistic and, at the same time, most tragic works. As is the case with verses by Anacreon or Omar Khayyám, "*Poema del otoño*" is an exhortation to live, an invitation to the sensual world, and—perhaps most of all—a vision of love as the means of approaching death with a glad heart. The poem is a satisfying adaptation of the *carpe diem* theme:

> *Gozad de la carne, ese bien*
> *que hoy nos hechiza,*
> *y después se tornará en*
> *polvo y ceniza.*

> *Gozad del sol, de la pagana*
> *luz de sus fuegos;*
> *gozad del sol, porque mañana*
> *estaréis ciegos.*

> *Gozad de la dulce armonía*
> *que a Apolo invoca;*
> *gozad del canto, porque un día*
> *no tendréis boca.*

> *Gozad de la tierra, que un*
> *bien cierto encierra;*
> *gozad, porque no estáis aún*
> *bajo la tierra.*

> [Enjoy the flesh, that good
> which today enchants us,
> and later turns into
> dust and ashes.

Enjoy the sun, the pagan
light of its fires;
enjoy the sun, because tomorrow
you will be blind.

Enjoy the sweet harmony
that invokes Apollo;
enjoy the singing, because one day
you will have no mouth.

Enjoy the earth that a
certain good encloses;
enjoy, because you are not yet
under the earth.]

In other words, Darío proposes total, universal enjoyment, but one compounded with an awareness of death, that irremediable human destiny, and a bitter taste of disappointment and tragedy in the face of the insurmountable mystery of existence. The last book of Rubén Darío's poetry published in his lifetime appeared in Madrid in 1914, under the title *Canto a la Argentina y otros poemas* [*Song to Argentina and Other Poems*]. This volume is really a compilation of verse written after *Poema del otoño y otros poemas*, the exception being the final poem, "*Gesta del coso*", which dates from 1890. Darío wrote the extensive "*Canto a la Argentina*" in 1910, to coincide with the centennial celebration of the independence of the Argentine Republic. The section "*Otros poemas*" includes a number of compositions with an amorous, philosophic, or religious theme, as well as others of a more topical nature. The poem "*La Cartuja*" ["The Charterhouse"], written on the island of Majorca, relentlessly swings like a pendulum between the spirit and the flesh. Many stanzas veer from the spiritual (what Darío would *like* to be) to the pagan (what, in fact, he *is*). In other words, Christian dualism:

Darme otra boca en que queden impresos
los ardientes carbones del asceta,
y no esta boca en que vinos y besos
aumentan gulas de hombre y de poeta.

Darme unas manos de disciplinante
que me dejen el lomo ensangrentado,

y no estas manos lúbricas de amante
que acarician las pomas del pecado.

[To give myself another mouth stamped
with the burning coals of the ascetic,
and not this mouth where wines and kisses
increase the gluttony of man and of poet.

To give myself a pair of flagellant's hands
that leave my back bloody,
and not these lewd lover's hands
that caress the apples of sin.]

And in the end, the hope of redemption, now all the more tragic for being felt so necessary. Another significant piece in this book is the concluding poem, "*Gesta del coso*," the dialogue of an ox and a bull just before the latter goes out to fight and die in the ring. It seems as if Darío divides himself between the two animals in order to underscore the anguish of death, that inevitable and tragic destiny of being. Several poems, although unpublished in book form, are nevertheless significant in any assessment of Darío's poetry. For this anthology we have selected a few such works to show both the remarkable quality of Rubén Darío as a poet and the overarching unity of his poetry. To a great extent poems like "*Aúm*" ["Om"], "*Reencarnaciones*" ["Reincarnations"], "*La tortuga de oro . . .*" ["The Golden Tortoise . . ."], or "*En las constelaciones*" ["In the Constellations"] carry on the rich philosophical subject matter seen in previous poems. Other uncollected poems resort to themes of the Hispanic race ("*Español*" or "Spanish"), of love, or of the social fabric, in all of which we discern the poetic mastery of their author.

RUBÉN DARÍO IN THE CONTEXT OF HISPANIC POETRY

As much as Spanish poetry of the Golden Age served as a model for the rest of Europe, Spanish-language poetry—on both sides of the Atlantic—fell short of European poetry in general, and French poetry in particular, in the eighteenth and nineteenth centuries. We would venture to claim, in fact, that none of those poets considered exceptional in Spain and Spanish America in the nineteenth century—Espronceda, Zorrilla, Campoamor,

Núñez de Arce, Heredia, and Hernández—could measure up to the best
poets writing in France during these same years: first Hugo and Baudelaire,
and later Verlaine, Rimbaud, and Mallarmé. It was in the midst of such
conditions of sterility—relieved in Spain by G. A. Bécquer and Rosalía de
Castro, the latter all but forgotten in her day—that so-called *modernismo*
made its appearance in Spanish America during the last decades of the nine-
teenth century and revolutionized the very concept of poetry. As stated
previously, in the search for new forms of expression, poets shifted their
view to Parnassian and French symbolist poetry. Along with Darío, the
important Spanish American *modernista* poets were—in the ebb and flow of
the movement—Julián del Casal and José Martí of Cuba; Salvador Díaz
Mirón, Manuel Gutiérrez Nájera, and Amado Nervo of Mexico; José
Asunción Silva of Colombia; José Santos Chocano of Peru; Ricardo Jaimes
Freyre of Bolivia; Delmira Agustini and Julio Herrera y Reissig of Uruguay;
and Leopoldo Lugones of Argentina. As for *modernista* poets in Spain, any
list must include Juan Ramón Jiménez, the brothers Antonio and Manuel
Machado, Manuel Reina, Salvador Rueda, Ricardo Gil, Francisco Villaespesa,
Eduardo Marquina, Ramón del Valle-Inclán, Enrique Díez-Canedo, and Tomás
Morales. More than all the rest, of course, Rubén Darío stands as the cor-
nerstone of the new esthetics. As the principal figure in a movement of
poetic reform, Darío truly infused Spanish-language poetry with fresh ideas
and, in consequence, ushered in contemporary Hispanic poetry. Although
a considerable number of critics may still view Bécquer as the first modern
poet in Spanish, to our way of thinking Darío must be recognized as the
poet with whom contemporary Spanish-language poetry begins. Notwith-
standing the affection and respect which Bécquer richly deserves, the truth
is that Rubén Darío's poetic voice owes little or nothing to him beyond
some early verses, the *Rimas* of 1887, one of the feeblest efforts of the Nica-
raguan. The metaphysical dimension so fundamental in Darío, for example,
is far less central to Bécquer's world. The tale of love in some of the best
compositions of Bécquer's own *Rimas*, published in 1871, strikes the mod-
ern reader as quaint and almost maudlin when compared to Darío's an-
guished message in the poem "*Lo fatal*" from *Cantos de vida y esperanza*,
raising the central problem of thought in the twentieth century: the begin-
ning and the end, life and death, the enigma and mystery of being human.
The difference between Bécquer and Darío in poetic stature and sheer out-
put—it must be admitted—is rather striking. Bécquer's slim volume of verse
must be weighed against the number and diversity of Darío's published

works. Moreover, Bécquer's impact on the influential poets of Spain's *Grupo del 27* [Generation of 1927] pales in comparison to Darío's. No less a poet than the Nobel Prize winner Juan Ramón Jiménez—who respected, admired, and began his career writing *modernista* verse—serves as a direct link between Darío and the *Grupo del 27*. But even beyond the historical presence of Jiménez, the poets of that group learned to make poetry by reading Darío, as may be seen in the youthful works of Vicente Aleixandre and Dámaso Alonso. It should go without saying that Federico García Lorca owes much to *modernismo* and to Rubén Darío. The same may be said of all Spanish and Spanish American poets of the twentieth century. Thanks to Darío's example, poets on both sides of the Atlantic developed a modern concern for the acoustic, lexical, and grammatical aspects of poetry which had received little attention since the death of Francisco de Quevedo in 1645. More plainly in the case of Spanish America, the fracturing of poetic language and the extraordinary rupture in poetic conventions—seen in the Peruvian poet César Vallejo, for example—are truly indebted to the formal concerns of *modernista* poetry and particularly to Darío. Vallejo's *Los heraldos negros*, published in 1918, is a clear offshoot of *modernista* esthetics. Beyond exclusively formal considerations, writers have come to draw upon the very concepts framed by such esthetics. For example, the Mexican poet Octavio Paz's vision of poetry as queen of the arts and of human activities, grows out of the glorification with which *modernista* poets in general, and Rubén Darío in particular, attempted to sanctify the genre. A demonstration of Darío's prominence in Spanish American poetry of the twentieth century took place in Varadero, Cuba, in January 1967, the centennial observance of the poet's birth. In this "Rubén Darío Encounter" various critics and poets endeavored to gauge for themselves the vital elements as well as the dead ends in Darío's literary production. The poets meeting there—Nicolás Guillén, Mario Benedetti, Eliseo Diego, Roberto Fernández Retamar, Heberto Padilla, among others—comprised in person a veritable anthology of the most recent Spanish American poetry. They concluded that their work, like that of most Spanish American poets of the twentieth century, can be seen as an outcome of efforts undertaken at the end of the previous century by *modernista* poets and, first and foremost, by Rubén Darío. The 1967 meeting, the results of which were published in the journal *Casa de las Américas*, bears witness to the preponderance of Spanish American writers who see themselves as Rubén Darío's poetic heirs.[5] Also in 1967, Raimundo Lida examined Darío's legacy in contemporary poetry and concluded:

Que a medio siglo de su muerte Rubén pueda suscitar todavía desprecios y elogios injustos, que hasta pueda impacientar a algunos verdaderos poetas, todo eso nos dice cuán cerca de nosotros está . . . La modernidad de Rubén Darío es, en nuestros tiempos, más tangible que nunca. Rubén sigue provocando herejías, discrepancias y ambigüedades: sigue siendo un gran poeta aún hoy inexplorado y difícil, aún hoy pregunta viva.

[The fact that Darío can still rouse unwarranted contempt and praise half a century after his death, that he can even exasperate some genuine poets, suggests just how close to us he remains . . . The modernity of Rubén Darío is, in our times, more tangible than ever. Darío continues to stir up dissension, disagreements, and ambivalence: he contines to be a great poet who even now is difficult and uncharted, even now an open question.][6]

These words lose none of their validity in the context of poetry at the end of the twentieth century: we certainly remain indebted to Darío for having revolutionized Spanish-language poetry, as much in its *form* of expression as in the *universe* of that expression. Formally, Darío's painstaking control of the word and its music is irrefutable. He was also one of the first poets in the language to use modern free verse. Although Juan Ramón Jiménez would establish free verse in Spain with the publication of *Diario de un poeta reciencasado* [*Diary of a Newlywed Poet*] in 1917, a year after Darío's death, the fact remains that Darío had already employed it in poems such as "*Heraldos*" ["Heralds], "*Salutación del optimista*" ["The Optimist's Salutation"], "*¡Aleluya!*" ["Hallelujah!"], and others. In terms of form, then, Darío—along with José Martí—led the way with free verse, so prevalent in twentieth-century Hispanic poetry. Thematically, Darío was first to deal poetically with certain subjects of universal relevance, carving out a profound metaphysical and existential dimension that would persist in Miguel de Unamuno, Antonio Machado (and, to a lesser degree, his brother Manuel), and Juan Ramón Jiménez, the principal Spanish poets in the opening years of the twentieth century. José Hierro, one of the representative poets of the Spanish postwar era, asserted in a 1967 article: "*La poesía española de hoy es inimaginable sin la existencia de Rubén. Juan Ramón, Machado, la generación del 27, no se conciben sin el antecedente rubeniano.*"[7] ["The Spanish poetry of today would be unimaginable without Darío. Juan Ramón {Jiménez}, {Antonio} Machado, the Generation of 1927 are inconceivable without him as the precursor."]

Somewhat later, Carlos Bousoño—another poet of Hierro's generation—wrote in a tribute on the centennial of the publication of *Azul* . . . :

Rubén Darío es el origen verdadero de toda la poesía en lengua española de nuestro siglo . . . Bécquer, repito, al no haber roto con el Romanticismo, pese a su nacimiento tan tardío (1836), no pudo situar la poesía hispana a la altura de los tiempos, y, por tanto, no pudo traer para ella la necesaria renovación.[8]

[Rubén Darío is the real source of all the Spanish-language poetry of this century . . . Bécquer, I repeat—for not having broken with Romanticism, despite being born so late (1836)—, could not lift Hispanic poetry to the high standard of that period, and thus could not bring to it the necessary renovation.]

Alberto J. Pérez concluded a 1989 article by asserting that Darío "*hizo posible nuestra modernidad poética . . . Debemos reconocerlo como el fundador de nuestra modernidad literaria.*"[9] [Darío "made our poetic modernity possible . . . We ought to recognize him as the founder of our literary modernity."] Darío's influence on the Spanish poets of the early postwar era is noted by Manuel Mantero in his exhaustively researched study *Poetas españoles de posguerra*, in which he states that "*el árbol genealógico de la poesía contemporánea española se nutre también en tierras rubendarianas. Por lo pronto, la canalización expresiva proviene de él.*"[10] ["The genealogical tree of contemporary Spanish poetry is also rooted in the soil of Rubén Darío. For the time being, its pathways of expression have originated in him."] Any number of works from the postwar period will reveal Darío's presence, making it a simple matter to list the Spanish poets indebted to him in some way: Blas de Otero, José Hierro, Ramón de Garciasol, Victoriano Crémer, Camilo José Cela, José García Nieto, and Carmen Conde, among many others. We realize that such an assessment is by no means unanimous. Luis Cernuda, a member of the *Grupo del 27* with an opposing view, has severely attacked Darío, most notably in a 1960 article.[11] In response, Ernesto Mejía Sánchez refuted several of Cernuda's allegations and demonstrated the lasting significance of Darío.[12] In recent years a general affinity with Cernuda's opinions seems to have impeded a fair reading of Darío by certain Spanish poets. Because of this, there is a need to restore and reevaluate both him and his works. Back in the centennial year of 1967, Andrés Rodríguez Ramón devoted an entire book, aptly titled *Permanencia de Rubén Darío* [*Rubén Darío's Permanence*], to a demonstration of the actuality of Darío and his poetry. Rodríguez Ramón patiently pored over the previous twenty-five years of *ABC*, the Madrid daily, in search of Darío's presence. The investigation uncovered the fact that Darío's best-known verses, and even some lesser known, not only appear to have been memorized by large segments of the public, but are often quoted by journalists and commentators in observing various conventions, realities, and abstractions of our way of life. In Rodríguez Ramón's own words: "*No hay en el idioma español, ni en ninguno de los demás idiomas, otro escritor que haya dejado una huella tan perdurable y tan honda en nuestro pensar y en nuestro sentir.*"[13] ["There is no other writer in Spanish, nor in any other language, who has left such a profound and enduring stamp on our thinking and on our feeling."] Now on the threshold of the twenty-first century, and for the foreseeable future, Darío's modernity is, for us, indisputable. His presence is not only alive and well in contemporary Hispanic poetry, but may be found in all of today's literature. For all the above, then, Rubén Darío's poetry must be considered one of the most enthralling literary efforts ever produced in the Spanish language. His strengths as a word artist, above and beyond any literary school or style, elevate him to the pinnacle of the world's greatest writers of lyrical poetry. Yet today the need arises for a scrupulously edited volume of Darío's complete poems because many editions of his works—including those anthologies considered classic, publications of quite recent date, and even editions of specific books offered by reputable publishers—are demonstrably flawed with respect to textual fidelity, thus endangering the transmission of Darío's legacy. It is precisely in the matter of fidelity to the text where we have wished to take special care in the making of the *Selected Poems of Rubén Darío*, presented here.

NOTES

1. Guillermo Díaz-Plaja, *Modernismo frente a noventa y ocho* (Madrid: Espasa-Calpe, 1951); Juan Ramón Jiménez, *El modernismo: Notas en torno de un curso (1953)*, ed. Ricardo Gullón (Mexico: Aguilar, 1962); Max Henríquez Ureña, *Breve historia del modernismo* (Mexico: Fondo de Cultura Económica, 1954); Ricardo Gullón, *Direcciones del modernismo* (Madrid: Gredos, 1964); Ned J. Davison, *The Concept of Modernism in Hispanic Criticism* (Boulder: Pruett, 1966); Ivan A. Schulman, *Génesis del modernismo* (Mexico: Colegio de México, 1966); Ivan A. Schulman, *El modernismo hispanoamericano* (Buenos Aires: Centro Editor de América Latina, 1969); Ivan A. Schulman, *Nuevos asedios al modernsimo* (Madrid: Taurus, 1987); Angel Rama, *Rubén Darío y el modernismo (Circunstancia socioeconómica de un arte americano)* (Caracas: Ediciones de la Biblioteca de la Universidad Central de Venezuela, 1970); Angel Rama, *Las máscaras democráticas del modernismo* (Montevideo: Fundación Angel Rama, 1985); Robert R.

Anderson, *Spanish American Modernism: A Selected Bibliography* (Tuscon: University of Arizona Press, 1970); Homero Castillo, ed., *Estudios críticos sobre el modernismo* (Madrid: Gredos, 1974); Lily Litvak, ed., *El modernismo* (Madrid: Taurus, 1975); Françoise Perús, *Literatura y sociedad en América Latina: El modernismo* (Havana: Casa de las Américas, 1976); Saúl Yurkevich, *Celebración del modernismo* (Barcelona: Tusquets, 1976); Noé Jitrik, *Las contradicciones del modernismo: Productividad poética y situación sociológica* (Mexico: Colegio de México, 1978); Rafael Gutiérrez Girardot, *Modernismo* (Barcelona: Montesinos, 1983); José Olivio Jiménez, ed., *Antología de la poesía modernista hispanoamericana* (Madrid: Hiperión, 1985); and Guillermo Carnero, ed., *El modernismo español e hispanoamericano* (Cordova: Diputación Provincial, 1987).

2. Gilbert Azam, *El modernismo desde dentro* (Barcelona: Anthropos, 1989); Iris M. Zavala, *Colonialism and Culture: Hispanic Modernisms and the Social Imaginary* (Bloomington: Indiana University Press, 1992); Richard Cardwell and Bernard McGuirk, *¿Qué es el modernismo?* (Boulder: Society of Spanish Studies, 1993); Graciela Montaldo, *La sensibilidad amenazada: Tendencias del modernismo latinoamericano* (Caracas: Editorial Planeta Venezolana, 1995); and Cathy Login Jrade, *Modernismo and Modernity* (Austin: University of Texas Press, 1998).

3. Ignacio M. Zuleta, *La polémica modernista: El modernismo de mar a mar (1898-1907)* (Bogota: Publicaciones del Instituto Caro y Cuervo, LXXXII, 1988); María Pilar Celma Valero, *La pluma ante el espejo (Visión autocrítica del "fin de siglo", 1888-1907)* (Salamanca: Ediciones de la Universidad de Salamanca, 1989).

4. Lysander Kemp, trans., *Selected Poems of Rubén Darío* (Austin: University of Texas Press, 1965).

5. *Casa de las Américas* VII, 42 (May-June 1967).

6. Raimundo Lida, "*Rubén y su herencia,*" *La Torre* XV, 55-56 (1967), 308.

7. José Hierro, "*La huella de Rubén en los poetas de la posguerra española,*" *Cuadernos Hispanoamericanos* 212-13 (1967), 367.

8. Carlos Bousoño, "*Lo que debemos a Rubén,*" *ABC Literario* 30 July 1988, iii.

9. Alberto Julián Pérez, "*La enciclopedia poética de Rubén Darío,*" *Revista Iberoamericana* 146-47 (1989), 338.

10. Manuel Mantero, *Poetas españoles de posguerra* (Madrid: Espasa-Calpe, 1986), 45.

11. Luis Cernuda, "*Experimento en Rubén Darío,*" *Papeles de Son Armadans* 19 (1960), 123-37.

12. Ernesto Mejía Sánchez, "*Rubén Darío, poeta del siglo XX,*" in *Cuestiones rubendarianas* (Madrid: Ediciones de la *Revista de Occidente*, 1970), 105-27.

13. Andrés Rodríguez Ramón, *Permanencia de Rubén Darío* (Charlotte: Heritage Printers, 1967), 4.

2

Justification and Originality of the
Present Anthology and Translation

Since Rubén Darío's death in 1916, efforts to compile his total literary output, and particularly his poetry, have been many. Besides the reissue of specific books, anthologies have appeared in great proliferation, some with poems not previously published. There have even been several editions of Darío's complete poetry, all of them flawed in some way. None can really be considered complete or in any sense critical editions with respect to texts and notes. This judgment includes Méndez Plancarte's editions, first published in 1952, and the later additions under Antonio Oliver Belmás for the "Centennial Edition" *(CE)* of 1967, despite its current standing as the most complete of all.[1] After 1967, various anthologies or partial editions of Darío's poetry continued to appear. Together with the reissue of the *CE*, the best-known and most-used edition of Darío's books of poetry is that of E. Mejía Sánchez (1977), although—however carefully edited—it still contains errors.[2] The many anthologies of Darío's poetry generally follow the published texts of previous editors, primarily Méndez Plancarte, Oliver Belmás, and Mejía Sánchez. Rarely if ever is the text actually checked against the first editions, much less the manuscripts. Consequently, until now practically all the anthologies of Darío's poetry have been lacking in textual accuracy and any real commitment to a faithful authorized text. Any comparison between the "Centennial Edition" and Darío's first editions clearly shows serious textual deficiencies. The poems constituting *Cantos de vida y esperanza. Los cisnes y otros poemas*, to choose a representative book, appear in the *CE* with a vast amount of mistakes when compared to the text of the first edition—mistakes repeated in later editions and anthologies. Such errata not only appear in the punctuation of certain verses, but also extend to indentations and spacing. However, most serious of all are numerous errors in wording, even in the case of titles. To illustrate this, we will cite a few poems from *Cantos de vida y esperanza. Los cisnes y otros poemas* that are found in our anthology. In the first poem of "*Los cisnes*," Darío wrote in verse 18: "*se mueren nuestras rosas, se agotan nuestras palmas*" ["our roses are killed off, our palm trees used up"]; and not, as the *CE* has it: "*se mueren nuestras rosas, se agostan nuestras palmas*" ["our roses are killed off, our palm trees fade away"] (648). In the section "*Otros poemas*," the word at the end of the sixth verse of "*Nocturno*" should not be plural, as in the *CE* (656), but singular— that is, *blasfemia* ["blasphemy"]—in order to rhyme with *bohemia* ["bohemian life"] and complete a *serventesio alejandrino*, just as it did in the first edition. In the fourteenth stanza of "*Canción de otoño en primavera*" we find another mistake in the *CE* reading:

> *¡Y las demás!, en tantos climas,*
> *en tantas tierras, siempre son,*
> *si no pretexto de mis rimas,*
> *fantasmas de mi corazón.*

> (659)

> [And the rest of them! in so many climes,
> in so many lands, they will always be,
> if not a pretext for my rhymes,
> phantoms of my heart.]

In the first edition, along with the absence of the initial exclamation mark [¡], we find the word *pretextos* ["pretexts"]—that is, the plural form—because it refers to *las demás* ["the rest of them"], also in the plural. This kind of typographical error, while not completely forgivable, is qualitatively minor since it alters the sense of the poem only slightly. But it does clearly show the unreliability of the *CE* (and of all editions that follow it) in providing an absolutely accurate text. Other mistakes are truly significant because they turn the poem upside-down. A good example of this is the sonnet "*Cleopompo y Heliodemo*" ["Cleopompus and Heliodemos"] the last tercet of which reads in the *CE*:

> *y en la pupila enorme de la bestia apacible,*
> *miran como que rueda en un ritmo invisible*
> *la música del mundo, Cleopompus and Heliodemos.*

> (672)

[and in the enormous pupil of the placid beast,
Cleopompus and Heliodemos watch the music of the world
rolling in an invisible rhythm.]

The final tercet of the original text is preceded by a colon at the end of the eleventh verse, rather than the semicolon that appears in the *CE*. More significantly, Darío had actually written *ritmo visible* ["visible rhythm"] in verse 13, and not *ritmo invisible* ["invisible rhythm"]. Another poem in the *CE*, "*De otoño*" ["In Autumn"] breaks down at the beginning of its second stanza: "*Yo, pobre árbol, produje, el amor de la brisa, / cuando empecé a crecer, un vago y dulce son*" ["I, a poor tree, produced the breeze's love, / when I began to grow, a vague and sweet sound"] (676). According to this reading, the poet-as-tree produces the breeze, which is at least misleading, since Darío had written in the first edition: "*Yo, pobre árbol, produje, al amor de la brisa, / cuando empecé a crecer, un vago y dulce son*" ["I, a poor tree, produced, out of love for the breeze, / when I began to grow, a vague and sweet sound"]. According to this far more understandable reading, what the poet produces is "a vague and sweet sound" in the company of the breeze which he loves. Mistakes in the *CE* are not confined to isolated verses; it is surprising to find them even in the titles of poems. According to the 1905 edition of *Cantos de vida y esperanza. Los cisnes y otros poemas*, for example, the title of "*La dulzura del ángelus . . .*" ["The Sweetness of the Angelus" . . .] needs to end with three ellipsis points. Mistakes are also found in the captions and dedications. In the 1905 edition, Darío dedicated his poem "*Canción de otoño en primavera*" ["Song of Autumn in Springtime"] thus: "*A Martínez Sierra*"; the *CE* later placed a "G." for Gregorio into the dedication. While we have no space to detail them here, textual mistakes are equally widespread in Darío's other books of poetry. What makes the problem acute is the fact that so many errors continue to turn up in new editions of Darío's work, whether editions of specific books or anthologies. A painstaking comparison of various editions, which we began to carry out some time ago, together with the examination of their editorial criteria, proves the lack of textual rigor on the part of almost all of Darío's editors, and in too many cases the small importance attached to textual fidelity. On occasion editors even try to "correct" Darío, assuming him to have muddled certain details, such as mythological beings, foreign expressions, and the like. Such modifications are dangerous since they often run the risk of altering the number of syllables in a verse and thus spoiling the rhythm of the poem.

Certain editors claim it impossible to resolve textual problems on two grounds: (1) not all manuscripts have been preserved and (2) Darío himself virtually neglected the editorial oversight of books published in his lifetime. It is not difficult to see through these claims. Even a cursory examination of the various Darío collections will turn up proofs and galleys of books corrected in his own hand—for example, *Prosas profanas y otros poemas*. Furthermore, Darío's correspondence with friends and editors frequently reveals a concern with having his poetry published in the form in which he had written it. And finally, while admittedly not overly involved in the particulars, he did have competent friends like Juan Ramón Jiménez who helped him compile, edit, and proof the editions of his poems, as happened with *Cantos de vida y esperanza. Los cisnes y otros poemas*. Such facts refute the notion of a poet utterly indifferent to the way his works were published. For obvious reasons, the source text for Darío's poetry should be, whenever possible, the preserved manuscripts; where these are lacking, first editions of his books should be considered authoritative. The prevalence of serious textual shortcomings in editions of Darío's poetry must, in and of itself, justify the appearance of the present anthology. We are well aware of the risk of criticizing editions considered as model texts even today. The easier course would have been to follow them. However, our task as editors of Darío is not so much the criticism of other editions, but the search for a text as faithful as possible to what the poet himself left us. Having authenticated the texts, we then set about selecting poems—significant, representative, or both—to translate into English. In the U.S. and other English-speaking countries, Darío has never enjoyed the recognition which he richly deserves as a poet of the first order. The primary reason would seem to be that Darío is not only a writer in a foreign language, but a poet. A majority of citizens today could not name the past or present poet laureate of the United States and would be hard-pressed to identify any foreign poet other than Shakespeare. (In the near future Darío may very well become more popular—or at least better known—as Hispanics become the largest U.S. minority.) Another reason for Darío's relative obscurity is the lack of a solid body of translations. English versions of individual poems turn up here and there; sometimes a handful of poems in translation appear in general anthologies of Hispanic or Spanish American poets. As the central figure of *modernismo*, of course, Darío does not escape the notice of U.S. scholars, many of whom find themselves forced to translate a verse or a stanza in support of their argument when writing in English. Poets have also discovered Darío in their search for fresh inspiration, and no small number of them have attempted to render a specific poem into English. Nevertheless, nowadays

Rubén Darío does not rank among the Hispanic poets most often translated into English, where instead we find Federico García Lorca, Octavio Paz, and, most obviously, Pablo Neruda. The last serious effort at a representative Darío anthology in English appeared in 1965. As pointed out at the start of this introduction, while Lysander Kemp's translations have served U.S. readers for over thirty years, any real scrutiny of his text reveals misreadings of the original Spanish, lapses in versification, and even cases of the translator imposing his own intentions on the original meaning.

We are grateful for the efforts of others and have on occasion compared our translations against theirs, not only with respect to meaning but with an eye—and ear—to the poetic result. For it seems to us that the failures in rendering a Darío poem into English are often due to a clash of meaning and poetics, especially poetic form, the devices of rhythm and rhyme. We will attempt here a brief illustration of aspects that prove particularly problematical when translating Darío. Regular English versification has come to depend on the number of metric feet, that is, a repeated unit of stress rhythms, traditionally the iambic, trochaic, anapestic, dactylic, and amphibrachic foot. Spanish verse, however, is measured by the number of syllables. (For the purpose of measuring a verse, these syllables are conventionally acoustic rather than simply lexical, involving such processes as synizesis, elision, cesural pause, etc.) The two systems—metric feet and syllables—rarely coincide. Thus, for instance, the prevalent Spanish hendecasyllable may well show an iambic *tendency* with stress falling on the second, fourth, sixth, eighth, and tenth syllables, but cannot in fact be considered as true iambic pentameter due to an extra syllable. The difference is even more pronounced with a rhythm based on three-syllable feet such as the anapestic, dactylic, and amphibrachic: not only does an eleven-syllable verse defy regular division into units of three syllables; the Spanish hendecasyllable must also follow a precise system of accentuation that precludes adherence to all but the iambic rhythm. Whereas the verse may be said to display an anapestic tendency when stress falls on the third and sixth syllables, the requisite stress on the tenth syllable must necessarily break the anapestic rhythm. Darío uses verse of almost every sort then known in Spanish poetry and does not hesitate to modify any traditional form to suit a particular need. Given the vastly different morphological-syntactical systems of English and Spanish, the translator can seldom follow Darío's rhythmic patterns while still retaining the sense and register of what Darío is saying. The best a translator can usually do, we found, is to follow Darío by analogy: in other words, to use a rhythmic flow of words in English to suggest to the reader Darío's rhythmic emphasis in a certain line or stanza. An example of this occurs in the famous "*Sonatina*" of *Prosas profanas*. Darío's verse is hypnotically anapestic: *La princesa está triste . . . ¿qué tendrá la princesa?* We discovered that another three-syllable rhythm better suited the English translation, and so replaced anapests with amphibrachs: The princess is sad . . . What is wrong with the princess? More often than not, unfortunately, it proved impossible to follow Darío's rhythm so closely, and we had to settle for some sort of regularity of accentuation akin to tumbling verse to suggest that Darío's original was composed of lines of the same length. Of all poets, Darío is justly famous for the musicality—the acoustic dimension—of his verse. His use of rhyme was extraordinary even in his time. For a sense of Darío's rhyme schemes, and how end rhyme, interior rhyme, and alliteration seem to crackle in chain reactions all over the page, the reader may think of the Edgar Allan Poe of "Annabel Lee" and "The Raven," though we believe that Darío has a more delicate touch despite the similarities of acoustic bravura. Although Darío certainly employed assonant rhyme, he much preferred consonance. There are intrinsic differences here as well between the languages: Spanish verses generally end with feminine rhymes, while the prevalence of the monosyllable in English produces an emphatic and at times singsong rhyme. As we have suggested, Darío was a master of rhyme, including *rima rica*, the difficult or unusual rhyme. Wherever rhyme was possible at all, we used it whether or not a regular scheme could be maintained. Often we made use of softer assonant rhymes or even near rhymes to give the reader a sense of the rhyming that goes on in the original. With a single exception—the sonnet "Venus"—we could not stick to Darío's form without gumming up the contents, resulting in a singsong counterfeit that would have left readers scratching their heads about why Darío should be considered a real poet. And here we arrive at the true question confronting every translator: given the impossibility of transferring a multifarious work—alive and well—from one language to another, what is the essence to be conveyed? Darío's genius never resided in one aspect or another, but in the whole. His best poems, whether the first or hundredth time we read them, have an air of inevitability about them in both form and content. Also a sense of being inevitably *his*, for there is no mistaking that unique voice: what he says and the way he says it. Having admitted the formal limitations of translating poetry, we decided to follow as closely as possible—and, we admit, subjectively—the voice we hear when reading Darío. That voice is what so many translations of Darío so often lack. We will mention here some recourses employed in our anthology that are usually absent in other translations. Our pursuit of Darío's analogous voice in English involved some rather drastic hyperbaton at times: Darío loved to twist and turn his syntax from verse to verse, and only sometimes for the sake of a rhyme or for emphasis. English grammar simply does not have the same elasticity as Spanish, but we stretched it as far as it would bear (and we hope no further than that) in pursuit of the original. The register of Darío's diction is an important element which many translators either overlook or choose to ignore. His choice of words is precise, leaving nothing to chance. For instance, in the opening line of a "*Nocturno,*" the poet writes: "*Los que auscultasteis el corazón de la noche,*" deliberately using the rare and rather technical verb *auscultar.* It so happens that a form of the same Latinate verb exists in English as well, and so we have rendered the line: "Those of you who auscultated the heart of the night," bowing to Darío's word choice. On the other hand, Lysander Kemp translates the line thus: "You that have heard the heartbeat of the night," employing the most common and general verb in English to describe the auditory sense; he attempts to hint at *auscultate* by changing *heart* to *heartbeat,* altering the text on two levels (87). This is tantamount to correcting the poet, something we have criticized Darío's editors for doing; the sin is worse in the case of a translator. Regardless of personal preference in our own writing, we have tried to reproduce the atmosphere of Darío's language as faithfully as possible. This includes the use of odd, artificially "poetic" words like *lymph* for a limpid stream, for example, when Darío does the same in Spanish with the equally artificial *linfa.* In a poet as wantonly eclectic as Darío, there is a general tendency to tone him down in translation. Yet by first depriving him of his acoustic elegance through the simple act of translation and then dumbing down his expressiveness for the sake of imagined readers without access to a dictionary, translators too often produce empty verses that fail even to hint at the richness and complexity of Darío. In the same vein, translators have routinely gutted the allusions—mythological, esoteric, exotic, historical—so essential to *modernista* esthetics. The motive is understandable enough: Darío's reading of classical myth, to give but one example, is often obscure even for a reader from a former province of the Roman Empire or one of its Spanish American heirs; for a reader from the U.S.—however knowledgeable—the classical world generally resonates far less than for those in Latin cultures. We have elected to reproduce as accurately as possible the allusive world of Darío's poetry and to include at the end of the anthology a glossary of terms, names, and events with which the reader may not be familiar. Since this anthology is not intended solely for readers with experience in Spanish or knowledge of Hispanic cultures, we have also included some information which a great number of readers may already know. We hope that the translations will encourage readers to come to know the real Rubén Darío in the original texts. It is well worth the effort. In terms of textual accuracy and poetry in translation, then, may the present anthology—by no means definitive—serve as a first step towards a pressing reevaluation of Darío, towards future critical editions of his poetry, and towards a renewed interest in translating his poems into English.

NOTES

1. Rubén Darío, *Poesías completas,* ed. Alfonso Méndez Plancarte, with Antonio Oliver Belmás (Madrid: Aguilar, 1967).
2. Rubén Darío, *Poesía,* ed. Ernesto Mejía Sánchez (Caracas: Biblioteca Ayacucho, 1977).

3

Textual Criteria for
This Edition

Darío published ten books of poetry in his lifetime. We include in this number *Azul* . . . (1888, 1890, and 1905), a volume that combines verse and prose, as well as the *Canto épico a las glorias de Chile* and the *Rimas*, which initially appeared not in book form, but in the *Certamen Varela* anthology. Darío's ten books of poetry, then, chronologically determine the order of this anthology, from *Epístolas y poemas* (*Primeras notas*) (1885, 1888) to *Canto a la Argentina y otros poemas* (1914). In addition to poems selected from Darío's ten books, we have included a section of his "Uncollected Poems"—works published separately in the journals and newspapers of the time. We saw no need for a section of Darío's unpublished verse. Since his death in 1916, there have been more than a few special issues of journals, not to mention articles and books, with offerings of unpublished poems and manuscripts. In 1988, Ricardo Llopesa presented a compilation of Darío's unpublished poems, and later, with José Jirón Terán and Jorge Eduardo Arellano, Llopesa brought out more unknown poems of Rubén Darío.[1] Therefore we include in the present anthology none of the unpublished poems that have recently appeared, since others are engaged in the enterprise. This anthology strives to be a representative sampling of Rubén Darío's poetry over a lifetime, all carefully translated into English. In our selection and translation we have not been guided by the standards of previous anthologies, but by our own personal sensibilities. We have always operated with independence in the matter of selection, while endeavoring to omit none of the poems considered essential or canonical works of Rubén Darío ("*Coloquio de los centauros*," "*Yo soy aquel* . . . ," "*Lo fatal*," "*Poema del otoño*," and others). Even though works before *Azul* . . . may be particularly lacking in quality when compared to later books, we deemed it necessary to give at least a sampling of most works. Nevertheless, as will be seen, the great Rubén Darío begins—in our opinion—with *Azul* . . . and reaches his height in *Cantos de vida y esperanza. Los cisnes y otros poemas.* Therefore, we have included the prose prologues which Darío wrote for both *Prosas profanas* and *Cantos de vida y esperanza* because they illuminate the poems in these books, and because the prose—let us note in passing—is excellent. For textual questions we have always followed the first editions of his books, which in any event were consulted at all times. The specific citation for each book may be found in our *Bibliography of Rubén Darío.* As previously noted, the sheer volume of editions, reprints, anthologies, and selections from Darío's poetic works has on occasion generated an alarming amount of mistakes and alterations that ought to be emended. Such problems will only be exacerbated as the number of editions grows, until textual accuracy becomes dubious at best. To reiterate, we have consulted the first editions of Darío's books in order to avoid textual inaccuracy: our anthology strives to purge such lapses through adherence to first editions and, where possible, to preserved manuscripts, thus insuring at the same time an accurate English translation of the relevant works. Our sole purpose is to offer an authorative text and translation to the reader, without notes of explanation or interpretation, while also including a glossary of terms and names for those who wish to consult it. Our anthology, then, means to be an instrument for reading Darío with the greatest reliability possible: it contains the pure text just as the poet conceived it and often supervised it, accompanied by an English translation that finally allows the public unfamiliar with Spanish to read the poetry of one of the most significant voices in modern literature. As a rule we have respected the punctuation signs which Darío left in his work, and if any have been changed, it was a question of an obvious mistake even in the first edition. We have respected the use of spacing, indentations, roman numerals, and other typographical peculiarities. The one thing we did change was the capital letter at the beginning of verses, which Darío employed in some of his books, but not all. We omitted the initial capitals feeling that the change would better suit our readers, who expect the lower-case where today's usage leads them to expect it. Similarly, although a book like *Canto a la Argentina y otros poemas* may capitalize the first verse of each poem (or the first words), we have done away with the practice for the sake of consistency and because it may well have been more the editor's idea than Darío's. Certain obsolete or foreign spellings have been retained for their esthetic value. Modernizing the spelling does away with unsuitable accent marks, as well as other peculiarities; thus we use *armonía* for *harmonía*, *hexámetro* for *exámetro*, and so forth. In modernizing the text we have always sought to be consistent. In the matter of question marks and exclamation points we have respected Darío's choice not to use at times the initial punctuation (the ¿ and ¡) in order to set himself apart from Spanish poets and to show his "French" spirit of independence. If, as in the case of *Prosas profanas*, there are differences in the use of exclamation points between the 1896 and the 1901 editions, we have always followed the latter because it includes additional poems. In the case of poems selected from *Azul . . .* , we have followed the text of the third edition (Buenos Aires: Biblioteca de "La Nación," 1905, 139-86), since it is the edition which Darío considered definitive, as he himself pointed out in *Historia de mis libros* [*History of My Books*] when talking about *Azul . . .* Likewise, we have consulted the manuscripts of several of Darío's poems. Particularly in the case of *Cantos de vida y esperanza. Los cisnes y otros poemas*, we have checked the manuscript poems against the text of the first edition; the variants—basically punctuation—are minimal, and we have usually opted for the text of the first edition, since it was supervised by Juan Ramón Jiménez at the express desire of Darío himself. For poems not published in book form we have presented the text that seemed to us most reliable after comparing various editions of Darío's poetry: specifically the volume of poetry included in Darío's complete works, published by Afrodisio Aguado,[2] as well as the previously cited "Centennial Edition" published by Aguilar and the volume of Darío's poetry edited by the Biblioteca Ayacucho. The reader is reminded to regard the textual accuracy of these editions with a skeptical eye. In conclusion, we hope to offer here an anthology and translation of Rubén Darío's poetry faithful to the text which he himself envisioned. It is a body of work that remains today one of the most vital, most modern, and enduring manifestations of lyrical poetry written in the Spanish language. The task attempted in our *Selected Poems of Rubén Darío: A Bilingual Anthology* may shed valuable light on Darío's poetry. It is hoped that our efforts will also help students and specialists of comparative literature approach this poetry as a testimonial to one of the greatest voices in the history of Western literature.

NOTES

1. Ricardo Llopesa, ed., *Rubén Darío. Poesías inéditas* (Madrid: Visor, 1988); also R. Llopesa, J. E. Arellano, and J. Jirón Terán, eds., *Rubén Darío. Poesías desconocidas completas* (Altea: Ediciones Aitana, 1994).
2. Rubén Darío, *Obras completas*, ed. M. Sanmiguel Raimúndez (Madrid: Afrodisio Aguado, 1950-1955), vol. 5 (*Poesía*).

4

The Life of Rubén Darío
at a Glance

1867   Félix Rubén García Sarmiento—afterwards known as "Rubén Darío"—is born 18 January in Metapa (today Ciudad Darío), Nicaragua, and is baptized 3 March.

1868   Darío is raised in a home filled with quarrels between his parents, who soon separate.

1869   His mother, Rosa Sarmiento, leaves for Honduras with the boy Rubén. They suffer poverty. Relatives take over his care.

1870-72   Childhood with his adoptive parents, great-uncle Colonel Félix Ramírez and great-aunt Bernarda Sarmiento de Ramírez. The boy is enrolled in a nursery school in León, Nicaragua.

1873-76   As a student in the León public school, Darío learns to write verse with his teacher Felipe Ibarra.

1877   A rich uncle pays for studies at a private academy. Owing to a quarrel between Darío and his cousin, the uncle stops payment and Darío drops out of school.

1878-80   In the Church of the *Recolección* he studies Greek and Latin classics with the Jesuits. He writes and publishes poems.

1881   In León he comes into contact with the Polish intellectual José Leonard y Bertholet, who will greatly influence Darío's education. He travels to El Salvador, where he meets Francisco Gavidia.

1882   Given the fame of young Darío, the Nicaraguan government decides to defray the cost of Rubén's education. However, he never receives the promised aid. In August his friends convince him to break with his fiancée Rosario Murillo.

1883	The young Darío makes various public appearances and gives readings of poems. He carries on his affair with Rosario.
1884	Darío writes for the Managua press and works as a clerk in the office of Nicaraguan president Adán Cárdenas. Some of Darío's reviews begin appearing in the local press.
1885	He works at the National Library in Managua, reading Spanish classics in Rivadeneyra's *Biblioteca de Autores Españoles* [*Library of Spanish Authors*]. He prepares *Epístolas y poemas* for publication.
1886	With two partners Darío becomes manager of the daily *El Imparcial* of Nicaragua. Disillusioned with his fiancée Rosario Murillo for her relationship with a local politician, he embarks for Chile. He goes to Valparaíso and then to Santiago. He contributes creative pieces and theater reviews to the daily *La Época* of Santiago. He meets Pedro Balmaceda Toro, son of the president of Chile.
1887	He is named customs inspector in Valparaíso, a post he accepts for economic reasons. He participates in the *Certamen Varela* in the categories of lyrical and epic poetry, submitting *Rimas* and *Canto épico a las glorias de Chile*, respectively. The latter receives an award and *Rimas* an honorable mention. Both works are published the same year in an anthology of poems by participants in the *Certamen Varela. Abrojos*, a book of poems, appears.
1888	The 1885 edition *Epístolas y poemas* now appears with a different cover and title: *Primeras notas*. The first edition of *Azul . . . .* also appears in Valparaíso. His father, Manuel García, dies.
1889	Darío leaves Valparaíso for Nicaragua. He goes to El Salvador, where the Salvadoran president appoints him manager of the daily *La Unión*, devoted to notions of a political Central American union.
1890	Civil marriage to Rafaela Contreras Cañas on 21 June. Darío is manager and owner of the daily *El Correo de la Tarde*. His benefactor, the Salvadoran president, is assassinated the day after Darío's wedding. Darío leaves for Guatemala. The second edition of *Azul . . .* appears.
1891	In Guatemala with his wife and mother-in-law. A religious wedding with Rafaela takes place 11 February. He travels to

Costa Rica, where his first son—Rubén Darío Contreras—is born in November. The daily *El Correo de la Tarde* is suppressed.

1892 As Secretary of the Nicaraguan Delegation he attends the festivities in Spain for the Fourth Centennial of the Discovery of America. On 29 July he stops in Cuba, where he meets Julián de Casal in Havana. In August he arrives at La Coruña and goes on to Madrid. In November he returns to America with stops in Havana and Cartagena de Indias.

1893 Rafaela Contreras dies 26 January. The poet is distraught, and on 8 March marries Rosario Murillo in Managua, falling into a trap set by Rosario and her brother Andrés Murillo. In April he is named Consul General of Colombia in Buenos Aires. He goes to New York in May, where he meets José Martí. He leaves for France on 2 July. In Paris he meets various French poets and artists, among them his revered Verlaine. On 13 August he is again in Buenos Aires, where he writes for *La Nación*.

1894 With Ricardo Jaimes Freyre he edits the *Revista de América* in Buenos Aires. Darío takes part in the Athenaeum of the Argentine capital and constantly frequents the bohemian nightlife of Buenos Aires.

1895 His mother dies 5 May in El Salvador. He loses the post of Colombian Consul in Buenos Aires and continues to live off journalism.

1896 He is named Secretary to the Postal Director of Buenos Aires. The first edition of *Prosas profanas y otros poemas* appears in December.

1897 Rosario Murillo, legally Darío's wife, continues to pursue him even as he evades her, refusing to accept her as a wife. He continues to write for Buenos Aires newspapers.

1898 He leaves for Spain as correspondent of the daily *La Nación* of Buenos Aires, covering the war between Spain and the United States.

1899 He arrives in Barcelona the first of January and later goes to Madrid. There he meets Francisca Sánchez, his companion from then on. In December he moves to Paris to report on the Universal Exposition.

1900 While Darío is in Paris, his first daughter Carmen is born; she

	dies the following year. In September he travels to Italy: Genoa, Turin, Pisa, Venice, Livorno, Rome, and Naples.
1901	He spends the summer in Europe with Francisca Sánchez. The second edition of *Prosas profanas y otros poemas* appears with additional poems.
1902	He maintains correspondence with Juan Ramón Jiménez and meets Antonio Machado in Paris.
1903	On 12 March he is named Nicaraguan Consul in Paris. Rubén Darío Sánchez—"Phocas"—is born; the boy dies scarcely a year later.
1904	With the aid of Juan Ramón Jiménez, Darío contributes to Spanish magazines (*Blanco y Negro*, among others) out of economic necessity. He travels to Gibraltar, Morocco, and Andalusia. From there he goes on to Europe (Germany, Austria, and Hungary).
1905	With the aid of Juan Ramón Jiménez the first edition of *Cantos de vida y esperanza. Los cisnes y otros poemas* appears in Madrid. He spends the summer in Asturias.
1906	He travels through Europe (Great Britain, Belgium, and other places). In June he leaves for Brazil as Secretary of the Nicaraguan Delegation at the Pan-American Conference in Rio de Janeiro. He goes to Buenos Aires and from there to Paris. In October his second son Rubén Darío Sánchez—"Güicho"—is born. In November he goes to the island of Majorca, Spain, where he continues to write.
1907	Rosario Murillo pursues him. On his first trip to Nicaragua in fifteen years he has a meeting with her. He attempts to divorce her without success. The first edition of *El canto errante* appears in Madrid. In December he is named Nicaraguan Minister to Spain.
1908	He returns to Europe in April and as Nicaraguan Minister to Spain he presents his credentials to King Alfonso XIII. However, he suffers economic hardship when no money is received from the Nicaraguan government.
1909	He travels to Italy and to Paris.
1910	José Madriz, the new president of Nicaragua, appoints him delegate to the festivities for the Centennial of Mexican Independence. However, the insurrection of Porfirio Díaz frustrates his trip. He returns to Europe. The first edition of *Poema*

del otoño y otros poemas appears in Madrid. For *La Nación* he writes "*Canto a la Argentina*" on the occasion of the Centennial of the Argentine Republic's Independence.

1911 He barely alleviates a period of deep economic hardship by contributing to *La Nación*. The brothers Alfredo and Armando Guido offer him a job as manager of the magazines *Mundial* and *Elegancias*, a post which Darío accepts. He travels to Hamburg.

1912 He begins a promotional campaign for the magazines *Mundial* and *Elegancias*. From April to November he visits Barcelona, Madrid, Lisbon, Rio de Janeiro, São Paulo, Montevideo, and Buenos Aires. He falls ill and returns to France.

1913 He goes to Barcelona, returns to Paris, and in October leaves for Valldemosa, Majorca, as guest of friends Juan Sureda and his wife. In Valldemosa Darío vacillates between a deep religious faith bordering on mysticism and bouts with alcohol. On 27 December he returns to Barcelona.

1914 In April he is still residing in Barcelona. In October he moves to New York on a pacifist voyage following the outbreak of the First World War. In New York he falls ill with pneumonia. The first edition of *Canto a la Argentina* is published in Madrid.

1915 He arrives in Guatemala on 21 May, invited by that country's president to write poems in his honor. He moves to Managua with his wife Rosario Murillo. His health further weakens. He spends Christmas with Rosario and his brother-in-law Andrés Murillo.

1916 Now seriously ill, he goes to León in January. He suffers from irreversible cirrhosis and is operated on twice without success. After receiving the last rites he dies on 6 February and is buried a week later.

5

Bibliography of
Rubén Darío

A la Unión Centroamericana. León: Tipografía de J. Hernández, 1883.

Oda. Al libertador Bolívar. Del héroe americano. San Salvador: Imprenta de la Ilustración, 1883.

Epístolas y poemas. (Primeras notas). Managua: Tipografía Nacional, 1885 and 1888.

Abrojos. Santiago de Chile: Imprenta Cervantes, 1887.

Emelina. Valparaíso: Imprenta y Litografía Universal, 1887. (In collaboration with Eduardo Poirier)

"*Otoñales (Rimas)*" and "*Canto épico a las glorias de Chile*" in *Certamen Varela. Obras premiadas y distinguidas*. Santiago de Chile: Imprenta Cervantes, 1887. Volume I (52-66 and 186-96).

Azul . . . Valparaíso: Imprenta y Litografía Excélsior, 1888. (Second edition, expanded, in Guatemala: Imprenta de "*La Unión*," 1890) (Definitive edition, in Buenos Aires: Biblioteca de "*La Nación*," 1905)

A. de Gilbert. San Salvador: Imprenta Nacional, 1889.

Prosas profanas y otros poemas. Buenos Aires: Imprenta de Pablo E. Coni e hijos, 1896. (Second edition, expanded, in Paris: Librería de la Viuda de Ch. Bouret, 1901)

Los raros. Buenos Aires: Tipografía "La Vasconia," 1896. (Second edition, expanded, in Barcelona: Maucci, 1905)

Castelar. Madrid: Rodríguez Serra, 1899.

España contemporánea. Paris: Garnier Hermanos, 1901.

Peregrinaciones. Paris: Librería de la Vda. de Ch. Bouret, 1901.

La caravana pasa. Paris: Garnier Hermanos, 1902.

Tierras solares. Madrid: Leonardo Williams, 1904.

Cantos de vida y esperanza. Los cisnes y otros poemas. Madrid: Tipografía de la Revista de Archivos, Bibliotecas y Museos, 1905.

Oda a Mitre (chapbook). Paris: Imprimerie A. Eymeaud, 1906.

Opiniones. Madrid: Fernando Fe, 1906.

El canto errante. Madrid: M. Pérez Villavicencio, 1907.

Parisiana. Madrid: Fernando Fe, 1907.

El viaje a Nicaragua. Madrid: Biblioteca "Ateneo," 1909.

Alfonso XIII (chapbook). Madrid: Biblioteca "Ateneo," 1909.

Poema del otoño y otros poemas. Madrid: Biblioteca "Ateneo," 1910.

Letras. Paris: Garnier Hermanos, 1911.

Todo al vuelo. Madrid: Renacimiento, 1912.

Canto a la Argentina y otros poemas. Madrid: Biblioteca Corona, 1914.

Muy siglo XVIII. Madrid: Biblioteca Corona, 1914.

La vida de Rubén Darío escrita por él mismo. Barcelona: Maucci, 1915.

Muy antiguo y muy moderno. Madrid: Biblioteca Corona, 1915.

Y una sed de ilusiones infinita. Madrid: Biblioteca Corona, 1916.

Cabezas. Buenos Aires: Ediciones Mínimas, 1916.

6
Selected Studies on
Rubén Darío

Abate, Sandro. *Modernismo, Rubén Darío y su influencia en el realismo mágico.* Bahía Blanca: Editorial de la Universidad Nacional del Sur, 1998.

Acereda, Alberto. *Rubén Darío, poeta trágico. (Una nueva visión).* Barcelona: Editorial Teide, 1992.

———, ed. *Rubén Darío. La creación, argumento poético y expresivo.* Barcelona: Anthropos, 1997.

Aguado Andreut, Salvador. *Por el mundo poético de Rubén Darío.* Guatemala: Editorial Universitaria, 1966.

Alemán Bolaños, Gustavo. *La juventud de Rubén Darío.* Guatemala: Editorial Universitaria, 1958.

Alvarado de Ricort, Elsie. *Rubén Darío y su obra poética.* Montevideo: Biblioteca Nacional, 1978.

Ancona Ponce, Mario. *Rubén Darío y América. (El Nuevo Mundo, como realidad política en la poesía rubeniana).* Mexico: Parresia, 1968.

Anderson Imbert, Enrique. *La originalidad de Rubén Darío.* Buenos Aires: Centro Editor de América Latina, 1967.

Arellano, Jorge Eduardo. *Contribuciones al estudio de Rubén Darío.* Managua: Dirección General de Bibliotecas y Archivos, 1981.

———. *"Los raros." Una lectura integral.* Managua: Instituto Nicaragüense de Cultura, 1996.

———. *Rubén Darío en la Academia.* Managua: Academia Nicaragüense, 1997.

———, ed. *"Azul . . . " de Rubén Darío. Nuevas perspectivas.* Washington, D.C: Organización de los Estados Americanos, Col. "Interamer," 1992.

———. *Azul . . . y las literaturas hispánicas.* Mexico: Universidad Autónoma de México, 1990.

————. *Ciclo dariano 1991.* Managua: Instituto Nicaragüense de Cultura, Biblioteca Nacional Rubén Darío, 1992.

Armijo, Roberto. *Rubén Darío y su intuición del mundo.* San Salvador: Ed. Universitaria de El Salvador, 1968.

Barcia, Pedro Luis, ed. *Escritos dispersos de Rubén Darío recogidos de periódicos de Buenos Aires.* La Plata: Universidad de La Plata, 1968. Two volumes.

Battistessa, Angel J. *Rubén Darío: semblanza y florilegio.* Buenos Aires: Corregidor, 1988.

Cabezas, Juan Antonio. *Rubén Darío. Un poeta y una vida.* Madrid: Ediciones Morata, 1944.

Cabrales, Luis Alberto. *Provincialismo contra Rubén Darío.* Managua: Ministerio de Educación Pública, 1966.

Capdevila, Arturo. *Rubén Darío: "un bardo rei."* Buenos Aires: Espasa-Calpe, 1946.

Carilla, Emilio. *Una etapa decisiva de Rubén Darío (Rubén Darío en la Argentina).* Madrid: Gredos, 1967.

Castro, Humberto de. *Rubén Darío y su época.* Bogotá: Sociedad Editora de los Andes, 1967.

Concha, Jaime. *Rubén Darío.* Madrid: Ediciones Júcar, 1975.

Conde, Carmen. *Acompañando a Francisca Sánchez. (Resumen de una vida junto a Rubén Darío).* Managua: Editorial Unión, 1964.

Contreras, Francisco. *Rubén Darío, su vida y su obra.* Santiago de Chile: Ediciones Ercilla, 1937.

Cubeñas, José A. *Rubén Darío: restaurador de la conciencia de la armonía del mundo.* Long Island City: Nine Kings, 1975.

Del Greco, Arnold A. *Repertorio bibliográfico del mundo de Rubén Darío.* New York: Las Américas Publishing Co., 1969.

Derusha, Will. "El gran viejo de Rubén Darío." *Rubén Darío. La creación, argumento poético y expresivo.* Ed. Alberto Acereda. Barcelona: Anthropos, 1997. 141-45.

Díez de Revenga, Francisco J. *Rubén Darío en la métrica española y otros ensayos.* Murcia: Departamento de Literatura Hispánica, 1985

Ellis, Keith. *Critical Approaches to Rubén Darío.* Toronto: University of Toronto Press, 1974.

Escudero, Alfonso. *Rubén Darío, el modernismo y otras páginas.* Santiago de Chile: Editorial Nascimiento, 1985.

Ferreiro Villanueva, Cristina. *Claves de la obra poética de Rubén Darío*. Madrid: Ciclo Editorial, 1990.

Feustle, Joseph A. *Poesía y mística. Rubén Darío, Juan Ramón Jiménez y Octavio Paz*. Veracruz: Universidad Veracruzana, 1978.

Fiore, Dolores A. *Rubén Darío in Search of Inspiration; Greco-Roman Mythology in his Stories and Poetry*. New York: Las Américas Publishing Co., 1963.

Fogelquist, Donald L. *The Literary Collaboration and the Personal Correspondence of Rubén Darío and Juan Ramón Jiménez*. Coral Gables: University of Miami Press, 1956.

Garciasol, Ramón de. *Lección de Rubén Darío*. Madrid: Taurus, 1960.

————. *Rubén Darío en sus versos*. Madrid: Ediciones Cultura Hispánica del Centro Iberoamericano de Cooperación, 1978.

Ghiano, Juan Carlos. *Análisis de "Cantos de vida y esperanza."* Buenos Aires: Centro Editor de América Latina, 1968.

————. *Análisis de "Prosas profanas."* Buenos Aires: Centro Editor de América Latina, 1968.

————. *Rubén Darío*. Buenos Aires: Centro Editor de América Latina, 1967.

————, ed. *Rubén Darío: Estudios reunidos en conmemoración del centenario (1867-1967)*. La Plata: Universidad Nacional de La Plata, 1968.

Ghiraldo, Alberto. *El archivo de Rubén Darío*. Buenos Aires: Losada, 1943.

Giordano, Jaime. *La edad del ensueño: sobre la imaginación poética de Rubén Darío*. Santiago de Chile: Ed. Universitaria, 1971.

Gómez Espinosa, Margarita. *Rubén Darío, patriota*. Madrid: Ediciones Triana, 1966.

————. *Rubén Darío, poeta universal*. Madrid: Paraninfo, 1973.

González Gerth, Miguel and George D. Schade, eds. *Rubén Darío Centennial Studies*. Austin: University of Texas Press, 1970.

Guerrero, Julian N. and Lola Soriano de Guerrero. *Rubén Darío, escritor*. Managua: Imprenta Nacional, 1970.

————. *Rubén Darío: poeta místico y diplomático*. Managua: Editora Central, 1966.

Guerrero, Luis Beltrán. *Rubén Darío y Venezuela*. Caracas: Instituto Nacional de Cultura y Bellas Artes, 1967.

Henríquez Ureña, Max. *Rodó y Rubén Darío*. Havana: Sociedad Editorial Cuba Contemporánea, 1918.

Hernández de López, Ana María. *El "Mundial Magazine" de Rubén Darío.* Madrid: Beramar, 1989.

Herrero Mayor, Avelino. *El castellano de Rubén Darío; idioma y estilo.* Buenos Aires: Ministerio de Cultura y Educación, 1972.

———. *Rubén Darío; gramática y misterio en su poesía, con otras amenidades estilísticas.* Buenos Aires: Pleamar, 1967.

Hierro, José. *"La huella de Rubén en los poetas de la posguerra española."* *Cuadernos Hispanoamericanos* 212-13 (1967): 347-67.

Huezo, Francisco. *Últimos días de Rubén Darío.* Managua: Ediciones de la Academia Nicaragüense de la Lengua, 1963.

Hurtado Chamorro, Alejandro. *La mitología griega en Rubén Darío.* Avila: Ed. La Muralla, 1967.

Ingwersen, Sonya A. *Light and Longing: Silva and Darío: Modernism and Religious Heterodoxy.* New York: Peter Lang, 1986.

Jiménez, Juan Ramón. *Mi Rubén Darío (1900-1956).* Reconstruction, study, and critical notes by Antonio Sánchez Romeralo, ed. Moguer: Ediciones de la Fundación, 1991.

Jirón Terán, José. *Bibliografía general de Rubén Darío (Julio 1883-Enero 1967).* Managua: Universidad Nacional Autónoma de Nicaragua, 1967.

———, ed. *Quince prólogos de Rubén Darío.* Managua: Instituto Nicaragüense de Cultura, 1997.

Jrade, Cathy Login. *Rubén Darío and the Romantic Search for Unity: The Modernist Recourse to Esoteric Tradition.* Austin: University of Texas Press, 1983.

Larrea, Juan. *Intensidad del canto errante.* Cordova: Facultad de Filosofía y Humanidades, Universidad Nacional de Córdoba, 1972.

Ledesma, Roberto. *Genio y figura de Rubén Darío.* Buenos Aires: Eudeba, 1964.

Lida, Raimundo. *"Rubén y su herencia."* *La Torre* XV, 55-6 (1967): 287-308.

López Estrada, Francisco. *Rubén Darío y la Edad Media; una perspectiva poco conocida sobre la vida y obra del escritor.* Barcelona: Planeta, 1971.

Lorenz, Erika. *Rubén Darío: "Bajo el divino imperio de la música": Estudio sobre la significación de un principio estético.* Trans. Fidel Coloma González. Managua: Ediciones Academia Nicaragüense de la Lengua, 1960.

Loveluck, Juan, ed. *Diez estudios sobre Rubén Darío.* Santiago de Chile: Editora Zig-Zag, 1967.

Lozano, Carlos. *Rubén Darío y el modernismo en España (1888-1920). Ensayo de bibliografía comentada.* New York: Las Américas Publishing Co., 1968.

Maiorana, María Teresa. *Rubén Darío y el mito del centauro.* Buenos Aires: L'Amitié Guérinienne, 1961.

Mantero, Manuel. *"El yo existencial." La poesía del Yo al Nosotros.* Madrid: Guadarrama, 1971. 95-117.

————. *"¿Era masón Rubén Darío?" Heterodoxia* 6 (1989): 167-72.

Mapes, Erwin K. *L'influence française dans l'oeuvre de Rubén Darío.* Paris: Libraire Ancienne Honoré Champion, 1925.

Marasso, Arturo. *Rubén Darío y su creación poética.* Buenos Aires: Kapelusz, 1954.

Martín, Carlos. *América en Rubén Darío: aproximación al concepto de la literatura hispanoamericana.* Madrid: Gredos, 1972.

Martínez Domingo, José M. *Los espacios poéticos de Rubén Darío.* New York: Peter Lang, 1995.

Mejía Sánchez, Ernesto. *Cuestiones rubendarianas.* Madrid: Ediciones de la Revista de Occidente, 1970.

————, ed. *Estudios sobre Rubén Darío.* Mexico: Fondo de Cultura Económica, 1968.

Meza Fuentes, R. *De Díaz Mirón a Rubén Darío.* Santiago de Chile: Editorial Nascimiento, 1940.

Montiel Argüello, Alejandro. *Rubén Darío en Costa Rica.* San José: López Tercero, 1987.

————. *Rubén Darío en Guatemala.* Guatemala: Litografías Modernas, 1984.

Morales, Angel Luis. *La angustia metafísica en la poesía de Rubén Darío.* Río Piedras: Biblioteca de Extramuros, Universidad de Puerto Rico, 1967.

Morgado, Benjamín. *Rubén Darío. Ayer, hoy y siempre.* Santiago de Chile: Secretaría de Relaciones Culturales, 1988.

Noel, Martín Alberto. *Las raíces hispánicas en Rubén Darío.* Buenos Aires: Universidad Autónoma de Buenos Aires, 1972.

Oliver Belmás, Antonio. *Este otro Rubén Darío.* Barcelona: Aedos, 1960.

————. *Última vez con Rubén Darío: literatura hispanoamericana y española.* Madrid: Ediciones de Cultura Hispánica del Centro Iberoamericano de Cooperación, 1978.

Oyarzún, Luis, et al., eds. *Darío.* Santiago: Universidad de Chile, 1968.

Pantorba, Bernardino de. *La vida y el verbo de Rubén Darío: ensayo biográfico y crítico.* Madrid: Compañía Bibliográfica Española, 1967.

Patterson, Helen Wohl. *Rubén Darío y Nicaragua.* Washington: The Mitchel Press, 1963.

Paz, Octavio. "El caracol y la sirena." *Cuadrivio: Darío, López Velarde, Pessoa, Cernuda.* Mexico: J. Mortiz, 1965. 9-65.

Pedro, Valentín. *Rubén Darío.* Buenos Aires: Compañía Fabril Editora, 1965.

Peraza, José Antonio. *Las huellas masónicas de Rubén Darío.* Managua: Imprenta López y Cía., 1972.

Pérez, Alberto Julián. "La enciclopedia poética de Rubén Darío." *Revista Iberoamericana* 146-47 (1989): 329-38.

———. *La poética de Rubén Darío.* Madrid: Orígenes, 1992.

Porrata, Francisco E. and Jorge A. Santana, eds. *Antología comentada del modernismo.* Prol. Antonio Sánchez Romeralo. Sacramento: Explicación de Textos Literarios, Vol. VIII, Anejo I, 1974.

Quintián, Andrés R. *Cultura y literatura españolas en Rubén Darío.* Madrid: Gredos, 1973.

Rama, Ángel. "Introducción." *Rubén Darío. Poesía.* Ed. Ernesto Mejía Sánchez. Caracas: Biblioteca Ayacucho, 1977. ix-lii.

———. *Rubén Darío y el modernismo (Circunstancia socioeconómica de un arte americano).* Caracas: Ediciones de la Biblioteca de la Universidad Central de Venezuela, 1970.

Rodó, José Enrique. *Hombres de América: (Montalvo, Bolívar, Rubén Darío).* Barcelona: Cervantes, 1931.

Rodríguez Demorizi, Emilio. *Papeles de Rubén Darío.* Santo Domingo: Editorial del Caribe, 1969.

———. *Rubén Darío y Ecuador.* Quito: Casa de la Cultura Ecuatoriana, 1968.

———. *Rubén Darío y sus amigos dominicanos.* Bogotá: Ediciones Espiral, 1948.

Rodríguez Ramón, Andrés. *Permanencia de Rubén Darío.* Charlotte: Heritage Printers, 1967.

Saavedra Molina, Julio. *Bibliografía de Rubén Darío.* Santiago de Chile: Separatas de la "Revista Chilena de Geografía e Historia," 1946.

Salgado, María A. "Félix Rubén García Sarmiento, Rubén Darío y otros entes de ficción." *Revista Iberoamericana* 55, 146-47 (1989): 339-62.

Salinas, Pedro. *La poesía de Rubén Darío; ensayo sobre el tema y los temas del poeta.* Buenos Aires: Losada, 1948.

Salvador Jofre, Alvaro. *Rubén Darío y la moral estética.* Granada: Universidad de Granada, 1986.

Sánchez-Castañer, Francisco. *La Andalucía de Rubén Darío.* Madrid: Cátedra Rubén Darío-Universidad Complutense, 1981.

———. *Estudios sobre Rubén Darío.* Madrid: Cátedra Rubén Darío-Universidad Complutense, 1976.

Sánchez Reulet, Aníbal, ed. *Homenaje a Rubén Darío (1867–1967): Memoria del XIII Congreso Internacional de Literatura Iberoamericana (Primera Reunión).* Los Angeles: Centro Latinoamericano, University of California, 1970.

Schulman, Ivan, ed. *Recreaciones: ensayos sobre la obra de Rubén Darío.* Hannover: Ediciones del Norte, 1992.

———. *Rubén Darío: la tradición cultural y el proceso de modernización.* Hannover: Ediciones del Norte, 1990.

Seluja, Antonio. *Rubén Darío en el Uruguay.* Montevideo: Arca, 1998.

Sequeira, Diego Manuel. *Rubén Darío criollo o raíz y médula de su creación poética.* Buenos Aires: Guillermo Kraft Ltda., 1945.

———. *Rubén Darío en El Salvador. Segunda estada o atalaya de su revolución poética.* León: Editorial Hospicio, 1964.

Shaw, Donald L. "'Modernismo': A Contribution to the Debate." *Bulletin of Hispanic Studies* 46 (1967): 195-202.

Silva Castro, Raúl. *Génesis del "Azul . . ." de Rubén Darío.* Managua: Ediciones de la Academia Nicaragüense de la Lengua, 1958.

———. *Rubén Darío a los veinte años.* Madrid: Gredos, 1956. (Second edition, corrected and augmented. Santiago de Chile: Editorial Andrés Bello, 1966)

———. *Rubén Darío y su creación poética.* Santiago de Chile: Prensas de la Universidad de Chile, 1935.

Skyrme, Raymond. *Rubén Darío and the Pythagorean Tradition.* Gainesville: University of Florida, 1975.

Sol, Ildo. *Rubén Darío peregrino por la paz mundial.* Managua: Imprenta Democrática, 1962.

———. *Rubén Darío y las mujeres.* Managua: La Estrella de Nicaragua, 1948.

Torre, Guillermo de. *Vigencia de Rubén Darío y otras páginas.* Madrid: Guadarrama, 1969.

Torres, Edelberto. *La dramática vida de Rubén Darío*. Barcelona-Mexico: Grijalbo, 1966.

Torres Bodet, Jaime. *Rubén Darío. Abismo y cima*. Mexico: Fondo de Cultura Económica, 1966.

Torres-Rioseco, Arturo. *Casticismo y americanismo en la obra de Rubén Darío*. Cambridge: Harvard University Press, 1931.

Villacastín, Rosario M. *Catálogo-Archivo Rubén Darío*. Madrid: Editorial de la Universidad Complutense, 1987.

Various. "Rubén Darío." *Poesía. Revista Ilustrada de Información Poética* (Ministerio de Cultura de España) 34-5 (1991). (Monographic number)

Watland, Charles D. *La formación literaria de Rubén Darío*. Trans. F. Coloma. Managua: Publicaciones del Centenario de Rubén Darío, 1966.

———. *Poet-errant: A Biography of Rubén Darío*. New York: Philosophical Library, 1965.

Westbrook Harrison, Helene. *An Analytical Index of the Complete Poetical Works by Rubén Darío*. Washington: Microcard Editions, 1970.

Woodbridge, Hensley C. *Rubén Darío, a Selective, Classified, and Annotated Bibliography*. Metuchen: Scarecrow Press, 1975.

Ycaza Tigerino, Julio. *La palabra y el ritmo en Rubén Darío*. Managua: Editorial Impresiones Técnicas, 1987.

———. *Los Nocturnos de Rubén Darío*. Managua: Academia Nicaragüense de la Lengua, 1954.

———. *Los Nocturnos de Rubén Darío y otros ensayos*. Madrid: Ediciones de Cultura Hispánica, 1964.

Zambrana Fonseca, Armando. *Para leer a Darío: glosario básico*. Managua: Francisco Arellano Oviedo, 1998.

Zavala, Iris M. *Rubén Darío bajo el signo del cisne*. Río Piedras: Editorial de la Universidad de Puerto Rico, 1989.

Zepeda-Henríquez, Eduardo. *Estudio de la poética de Rubén Darío*. Managua: Comisión Nacional del Centenario, 1967.

Zuleta, Ignacio M. "Introducción biográfica y crítica." *Rubén Darío. Prosas profanas y otros poemas*. Madrid: Clásicos Castalia, 1983. 9-54.

———. *La polémica modernista: el modernismo de mar a mar (1898-1907)*. Bogotá: Publicaciones del Instituto Caro y Cuervo, LXXXII, 1988.

Part II:

Anthology

RUBÉN DARÍO

Prosas Profanas

y otros poemas

LIBRERÍA DE LA Vᴰᴬ DE C. BOURET

PARÍS | MÉXICO

23, Rue Visconti, 23 | 14, Cinco de Mayo, 14

1901

Propiedad del Editor.

Front cover of the 1901 edition of *Prosas profanas y otros poemas,* published in Paris and Mexico. This edition added several poems to the first 1896 edition of the same book published in Buenos Aires.

ABROJOS
(1887)

PUSO EL POETA EN SUS VERSOS . . .

Puso el poeta en sus versos
todas las perlas del mar,
todo el oro de las minas,
todo el marfil oriental;
los diamantes de Golconda,
los tesoros de Bagdad,
los joyeles y preseas
de los cofres de un Nabab.
Pero como no tenía
por hacer versos ni un pan,
al acabar de escribirlos
murió de necesidad.

PRIMERO, UNA MIRADA . . .

Primero, una mirada;
luego, el toque de fuego
de las manos; y luego,
la sangre acelerada
y el beso que subyuga.
Después, noche y placer; después, la fuga
de aquel malsín cobarde
que otra víctima elige.
Bien haces en llorar, pero ¡ya es tarde! . . .
¡Ya ves! ¿No te lo dije?

CUANDO LA VIO PASAR EL POBRE MOZO . . .

Cuando la vio pasar el pobre mozo
y oyó que le dijeron:—¡Es tu amada! . . .
lanzó una carcajada,
pidió una copa y se bajó el embozo.

THISTLES
(1887)

THE POET PUT IN HIS VERSES . . .

The poet put in his verses
all the pearls from the sea,
all the gold from the mines,
all the ivory from the East,
the diamonds of Golconda,
the treasures of Baghdad,
the jewels and the gems
from the coffers of a Nabob.
But as he had,
for making verses, not a crust to eat,
as soon as they were written
he died of need.

FIRST, A LOOK . . .

First, a look;
then the fiery touch
of hands; and then
      the rushing blood
      and the overwhelming kiss.
Later, night and pleasure; later, the flight
      of that spineless cheat
      with another victim to choose.
You do well to weep, but it's too late!
Now you know! Didn't I tell you?

WHEN THE POOR GUY SAW HER PASS . . .

When the poor guy saw her pass
and heard them tell him, "It's your lover!"
he burst out laughing,
ordered wine, and turned down his cape.

—¡Que improvise el poeta!
                    Y habló luego
del amor, del placer, de su destino . . .

Y al aplaudirle la embriagada tropa,
se le rodó una lágrima de fuego,
que fue a caer al vaso cristalino.
        Después, tomó su copa
¡y se bebió la lágrima y el vino! . . .

AMO LOS PÁLIDOS ROSTROS . . .

Amo los pálidos rostros
y las brunas cabelleras,
los ojos lánguidos y húmedos
propicios a la tristeza,
y las espaldas de nieve,
en donde, obscuras y gruesas,
            caen, sedosas,
            las gordas trenzas,
y en donde el amor platónico
huye, baja la cabeza,
mientras, temblando, se mira
la carne rosada y fresca.

"Let the poet improvise!"
                    And then he spoke
of love, of pleasure, of his fate . . .

And as the inebriated crowd applauded him
a fiery tear rolled down
and dropped in his crystalline glass.
Later, he took up his cup
and drank the tear and the wine!

I LOVE THE FACES PALLID . . .

I love the faces pallid,
and the hair dark brown,
the moist and languid eyes
predisposed to sadness,
and the snow-white backs
where, dark and thick,
          heavy tresses
          fall like silk,
and where platonic love
flees with bowed head
while trembling at the sight
of cool and rosy flesh.

CANTOS DE VIDA Y ESPERANZA

Darío's autograph in the cover of a copy of his book *Cantos de vida y esperanza* (1905). It reads: "Al Profesor L. S. Rowe. Simpáticamente, Rubén Darío. En el mar, junio 30, 1906." ("To Professor L. S. Rowe. Greetings, Rubén Darío. From the ocean, June 30, 1906.") Rowe was a professor at the University of Pennsylvania, where this copy of the book is still located.

Rimas
(1887)

Amada, la noche llega . . .

Amada, la noche llega,
las ramas que se columpian
hablan de las hojas secas
y de las flores difuntas.
Abre tus labios de ninfa,
dime en tu lengua de musa
¿recuerdas la dulce historia
de las pasadas venturas?
¡Yo la recuerdo! La niña
de la cabellera bruna,
está en la cita temblando,
llena de amor y de angustia.
Los efluvios otoñales
van en el aura nocturna,
que hace estremecerse el nido
en que una tórtola arrulla.
Entre las ansias ardientes
y las caricias profundas,
ha sentido el galán celos
que el corazón le torturan.
Ella llora; él la maldice,
pero las bocas se juntan . . .
En tanto, los aires vuelan
y los aromas ondulan,
se inclinan las ramas trémulas
y parece que murmuran
algo de las hojas secas
y de las flores difuntas.

El ave azul del sueño . . .

El ave azul del sueño
sobre mi frente pasa;
tengo en mi corazón la primavera
y en mi cerebro el alba.
Amo la luz, el pico de la tórtola,

74

Rhymes
(1887)

My love, the night has come . . .

My love, the night has come,
the swaying branches
speak of dry leaves
and dead flowers.
Open your nymph-like lips,
tell me in your muse-like tongue,
do you recall the sweet story
of long-ago pleasures?
I do! The girl
with the dark brown hair
is at a rendezvous, trembling,
full of love and anguish.
The first breath of fall
comes on the nocturnal breeze
shivering through the nest
where a turtledove coos.
Between the pangs of longing
and profound caresses,
the beau has felt jealousy
torturing his heart.
She cries; he curses her,
but the mouths come together . . .
Meanwhile, breezes fly
and aromas stir,
the quivering branches bend down
and seem to murmur
something about dry leaves
and dying flowers.

The dream's blue bird . . .

The dream's blue bird
passes over my brow;
in my heart I have the spring
and in my brain the dawn.
I love the light, the turtledove's beak,

75

la rosa y la campánula,
el labio de la virgen
y el cuello de la garza.
¡Oh, Dios mío, Dios mío! . . .
                    Sé que me ama . . .

Cae sobre mi espíritu
la noche negra y trágica;
busco el seno profundo de sus sombras
para verter mis lágrimas.
Sé que en el cráneo puede haber tormentas,
abismos en el alma
y arrugas misteriosas
sobre las frentes pálidas.
¡Oh, Dios mío, Dios mío! . . .
                    Sé que me engaña.

the rose and the campanula,
the virgin's lip,
and the heron's neck.
Oh my God, my God! . . .

                I know that she loves me . . .

Over my spirit falls
the night, black and tragic;
I seek the profound bosom of its shadows
to pour out my tears.
I know that in the skull there may be storms,
abysses in the soul,
and mysterious wrinkles
on pallid brows.
Oh my God, my God! . . .

                I know that she deceives me.

PRIMERAS NOTAS

DE

RUBEN DARIO

 MANAGUA—1888

TIPOGRAFIA NACIONAL—CALLE DE ZAVALA, NUM. 61.

Darío's first book of poetry, published in Managua in 1888. This is probably his weakest book, but it indicates his early poetic skills. An 1885 edition of this book disappeared after an earthquake.

Azul . . .
(1888, 1890, 1905)

PRIMAVERAL

Mes de rosas. Van mis rimas
en ronda, a la vasta selva,
a recoger miel y aromas
en las flores entreabiertas.
Amada, ven. El gran bosque
es nuestro templo; allí ondea
y flota un santo perfume
de amor. El pájaro vuela
de un árbol a otro y saluda
tu frente rosada y bella
como a un alba; y las encinas
robustas, altas, soberbias,
cuando tú pasas agitan
sus hojas verdes y trémulas,
y enarcan sus ramas como
para que pase una reina.
¡Oh, amada mía! Es el dulce
tiempo de la primavera.
       *

Mira: en tus ojos los míos:
da al viento la cabellera,
y que bañe el sol ese aro
de luz salvaje y espléndida.
Dame que aprieten mis manos
las tuyas de rosa y seda,
y ríe, y muestren tus labios
su púrpura húmeda y fresca.
Yo voy a decirte rimas,
tú vas a escuchar risueña;
si acaso algún ruiseñor
viniese a posarse cerca,
y a contar alguna historia
de ninfas, rosas o estrellas,
tú no oirás notas ni trinos,

BLUE . . .
(1888, 1890, 1905)

IN SPRING

Month of roses. My rhymes go
round, to the vast forest,
to gather honey and aromas
in flowers half-opened.
Come, my love. The great wood
is our temple; there flutters
and floats a holy perfume
of love. The bird flits
from tree to tree saluting
your pretty pink brow
like a daybreak; and as you pass,
the tall, robust, and proud
holly oaks wave
their trembling green leaves
and arch their branches the way
they would let through a queen.
Oh my love! It's the sweet
season of spring.

*

Look: within your eyes, mine:
give your hair to the wind
and let that ring of light,
savage and splendid, bathe the sun.
Grant that my hands may squeeze
yours of rose and silk,
and then laugh, and may your lips reveal
their fresh and dewy purple.
I will tell you rhymes,
you will listen smiling;
if by chance some nightingale
should come and perch nearby
and tell some story of old
about nymphs, or roses, or stars,
you will hear neither trill nor note,

81

sino enamorada y regia,
escucharás mis canciones
fija en mis labios que tiemblan.
¡Oh, amada mía! Es el dulce
tiempo de la primavera.
*

Allá hay una clara fuente
que brota de una caverna,
donde se bañan desnudas
las blancas ninfas que juegan.
Ríen al son de la espuma,
hienden la linfa serena;
entre polvo cristalino
esponjan sus cabelleras;
y saben himnos de amores
en hermosa lengua griega
que en glorioso tiempo antiguo
Pan inventó en las florestas.
Amada, pondré en mis rimas
la palabra más soberbia
de las frases de los versos
de los himnos de esa lengua;
y te diré esa palabra
empapada en miel hiblea . . .
¡Oh, amada mía! en el dulce
tiempo de la primavera.
*

Van en sus grupos vibrantes
revolando las abejas
como un áureo torbellino
que la blanca luz alegra;
y sobre el agua sonora
pasan radiantes, ligeras,
con sus alas cristalinas
las irisadas libélulas.
Oye: canta la cigarra
porque ama al sol, que en la selva
su polvo de oro tamiza,
entre las hojas espesas.

but will listen to my songs,
smitten and regal,
intent on my trembling lips.
Oh my love! It's the sweet
season of spring.

*

Over there a crystal–clear spring
bubbles up from a cave
where the white nymphs at play
are bathing naked.
They laugh at the sound of the foam,
cleaving the serene lymph;
in crystalline dust
they sponge their hair;
and they know anthems of love
in a beautiful Greek tongue
that in glorious days of yore
Pan invented in the glades.
My love, in my rhymes I will place
the most superb word
of the phrases of the verses
of the hymns of that tongue;
and I will tell you that word
dripping with Hyblaean honey . . .
Oh my love! in the sweet
season of spring.

*

In their vibrating groups
the bees begin circling
like a golden whirlwind
which the pure light gladdens;
and over the sonorous water
pass iridescent dragonflies,
radiant, nimble,
with crystalline wings.
Listen: the cicada sings
because she loves the sun
sifting down its gold dust
through the wood's thick leaves.

Su aliento nos da en un soplo
fecundo la madre tierra.
con el alma de los cálices
y el aroma de las yerbas.

             *

¿Ves aquel nido? Hay un ave.
Son dos: el macho y la hembra.
Ella tiene el buche blanco,
él tiene las plumas negras.
En la garganta el gorjeo,
las alas blandas y trémulas;
y los picos que se chocan
como labios que se besan.
El nido es cántico. El ave
incuba el trino, ¡oh, poetas!
de la lira universal
el ave pulsa una cuerda.
Bendito el calor sagrado
que hizo reventar las yemas,
¡oh, amada mía, en el dulce
tiempo de la primavera!

             *

Mi dulce musa Delicia
me trajo un ánfora griega,
cincelada en alabastro,
de vino de Naxos llena;
y una hermosa copa de oro,
la base henchida de perlas,
para que bebiese el vino
que es propicio a los poetas.
En el ánfora está Diana,
real, orgullosa y esbelta,
con su desnudez divina,
y en su actitud cinegética.
Y en la copa luminosa
está Venus Citerea
tendida cerca de Adonis
que sus caricias desdeña.
No quiero el vino de Naxos

Mother Earth breathes
on us a sigh fecund
with the soul of the calyxes
and the aroma of the herbs.

*

A bird is in that nest. See?
There are two: the male and female.
She has a white breast,
he has black feathers.
In their throat a warble,
the wings soft and fluttering,
and the beaks bumping
like kissing lips.
The nest is a canticle. The bird
incubates song—oh poets!—,
the bird plucks one chord
of the universal lyre.
Blessed be the sacred heat
that caused the yolks to hatch,
oh my love, in the sweet
season of spring.

*

My sweet muse Delight
brought me a Greek amphora,
engraved in alabaster,
full of wine from Naxos;
and a lovely cup of gold,
the base of it pearl-swollen,
so I would drink the wine
that is proper for poets.
On the amphora is Diana,
royal, proud, and lithesome
with her divine nudity
and in her cynegetics attitude.
And on the luminous cup
is the Cytherean Venus,
reclining by Adonis
who disdains her caresses.
I want no wine from Naxos,

ni el ánfora de ansas bellas,
ni la copa donde Cipria
al gallardo Adonis ruega.
Quiero beber del amor
sólo en tu boca bermeja,
¡oh, amada mía, en el dulce
tiempo de la primavera!

ESTIVAL

I

La tigre de Bengala,
con su lustrosa piel manchada a trechos,
está alegre y gentil, está de gala.
Salta de los repechos
de un ribazo, al tupido
carrizal de un bambú; luego a la roca
que se yergue a la entrada de su gruta.
Allí lanza un rugido,
se agita como loca
y eriza de placer su piel hirsuta.
                    *
La fiera virgen ama.
Es el mes del ardor. Parece el suelo
rescoldo; y en el cielo
el sol inmensa llama.
Por el ramaje obscuro
salta huyendo el canguro.
El boa se infla, duerme, se calienta
a la tórrida lumbre;
el pájaro se sienta
a reposar sobre la verde cumbre.
                    *
Siéntense vahos de horno;
y la selva indiana
en alas del bochorno,
lanza, bajo el sereno
cielo, un soplo de sí. La tigre ufana

nor the amphora with lovely handles,
nor the cup where Lady Cyprus
pleads with the dapper Adonis.
I want to sip at love
only in your wine-red mouth,
oh my love, in the sweet
season of spring.

In Summer

I

The Bengal tigress,
with stains here and there on her lustrous coat,
is all dressed up, genteel and blithe.
She leaps from the slope
of a cliff to the swarming
bed of bamboo; then to the rock
erect at the mouth of her grotto.
There she sends up a roar,
like a lunatic she twitches,
and pleasure makes her coat bristle.

*

The virgin beast loves.
It is the month of her heat. The earth
feels like embers; and the sun
flames immense in the sky.
Through the dark screen of branches
the kangaroo hops in flight.
The boa puffs up, sleeps,
warms itself in the torrid light;
the bird is perched
at rest upon the green height.

*

A furnace steam is felt;
in wings of swelter
the Indian jungle
launches, under the serene
sky, a sigh of consent. The haughty tigress

respira a pulmón lleno,
y al verse hermosa, altiva, soberana,
le late el corazón, se le hincha el seno.

*

Contempla su gran zarpa, en ella la uña
de marfil; luego toca
el filo de una roca,
y prueba y lo rasguña.
Mírase luego el flanco
que azota con el rabo puntiagudo
de color negro y blanco
y móvil y felpudo;
luego el vientre. En seguida
abre las anchas fauces, altanera
como reina que exige vasallaje;
después husmea, busca, va. La fiera
exhala algo a manera
de un suspiro salvaje.
Un rugido callado
escuchó. Con presteza
volvió la vista de uno y otro lado.
Y chispeó su ojo verde y dilatado
cuando miró de un tigre la cabeza
surgir sobre la cima de un collado.
El tigre se acercaba.

Era muy bello.
Gigantesca la talla, el pelo fino,
apretado el ijar, robusto el cuello,
era un don Juan felino
en el bosque. Anda a trancos
callados; ve a la tigre inquieta, sola,
y le muestra los blancos
dientes, y luego arbola
con donaire la cola.
Al caminar se vía
su cuerpo ondear, con garbo y bizarría.
Se miraban los músculos hinchados
debajo de la piel. Y se diría
ser aquella alimaña

breathes in deep,
finding herself beautiful, self-assured, sublime;
her heart throbs, her breast swells.

*

She beholds her great paw, the claw
of ivory; then she touches
the edge of a rock
and tastes and nips it.
Then she sees her flank,
lashed by her sharp tail
of white and black
and mobile and plush;
then the belly. All at once
she opens the wide maw, as a queen
exacts vassalage, haughty;
then she sniffs the air, looks about, walks. The beast
exhales something like
a savage sigh.
She harkened to a muffled
roar. At once
she swung her gaze from side to side.
And her green dilated eye sparked
at seeing the head of a tiger
loom above the crest of a ravine.
The tiger approached.

He was enticing.

Colossal of build, the hair fine,
the flank firm, the neck robust,
he was a feline Don Juan
in the woods. He strides along
without a sound; he sees the tigress restless, alone,
and shows her his white
teeth, and then gracefully raises
his tail like a mast.
As he walked his body
could be seen to ripple, audaciously jaunty.
The muscles visibly bulged
under his skin. And it might be said
that this beast was

un rudo gladiador de la montaña.
Los pelos erizados
del labio relamía. Cuando andaba,
con su peso chafaba
la yerba verde y muelle;
y el ruido de su aliento semejaba
el resollar de un fuelle.
El es, él es el rey. Cetro de oro
no, sino la ancha garra
que se hinca recia en el testuz del toro
y las carnes desgarra.
La negra águila enorme, de pupilas
de fuego y corvo pico relumbrante,
tiene a Aquilón; las hondas y tranquilas
aguas, el gran caimán; el elefante,
la cañada y la estepa;
la víbora, los juncos por do trepa;
y su caliente nido
del árbol suspendido,
el ave dulce y tierna
que ama la primer luz.

                         El, la caverna.

                *

No envidia al león la crin, ni al potro rudo
el casco, ni al membrudo
hipopótamo el lomo corpulento,
quien bajo los ramajes del copudo
baobab, ruge al viento.
                *

Así va el orgulloso, llega, halaga;
corresponde la tigre que le espera,
y con caricias las caricias paga
en su salvaje ardor, la carnicera.
                *

Después, el misterioso
tacto, las impulsivas
fuerzas que arrastran con poder pasmoso;
y ¡oh gran Pan! el idilio monstruoso
bajo las vastas selvas primitivas.

a crude gladiator from the mountain.
He licked the stiff whiskers
by his lip. When he moved,
his weight flattened
the lush green grass;
and the noise of his breath resembled
the chuffing of a bellows.
He is, he is the king. A golden scepter,
no, but the stout wide claw
that drives deep into the bull's neck
and rips apart the flesh.
The black enormous eagle, with pupils
of fire and dazzling curved beak,
has Aquilon; the deep and still
waters, the great alligator; the elephant,
the gorge and the steppe;
the viper as it climbs, the reeds;
and its warm nest
suspended from a tree,
the bird, tender and sweet,
that loves the early light.

He, the cavern.

*

He does not envy the lion his mane, nor the rude colt
his hoof, nor the burly
hippopotamus his corpulent haunch,
who—under the branches of the bushy
baobab—roars at the wind.

*

Thus walks the proud one, arriving, pleasing;
likewise the tigress who awaits him,
and in her savage ardor, the carnivore
returns caress for caress.

*

Later, the mysterious
touching, the wondrous
power driven by impulsive forces;
and—oh great Pan!—the monstrous idyll
under the vast primitive forest.

No el de las musas de las blandas horas,
suaves, expresivas,
en las rientes auroras
y las azules noches pensativas;
sino el que todo enciende, anima, exalta,
polen, savia, calor, nervio, corteza,
y en torrentes de vida brota y salta
del seno de la gran Naturaleza.

II

El príncipe de Gales va de caza
por bosques y por cerros,
con su gran servidumbre y con sus perros
de la más fina raza.

*

Acallando el tropel de los vasallos,
deteniendo traíllas y caballos,
con la mirada inquieta,
contempla a los dos tigres, de la gruta
a la entrada. Requiere la escopeta,
y avanza, y no se inmuta.

*

Las fieras se acarician. No han oído
tropel de cazadores.
A esos terribles seres,
embriagados de amores,
con cadenas y flores
se les hubiera uncido
a la nevada concha de Citeres
o al carro de Cupido.

*

El príncipe atrevido,
adelanta, se acerca, ya se para;
ya apunta y cierra un ojo; ya dispara;
ya del arma el estruendo
por el espeso bosque ha resonado.
El tigre sale huyendo
y la hembra queda, el vientre desgarrado.
¡Oh, va a morir! . . . pero antes, débil, yerta,

Not one with muses in the bland hours,
soft, expressive,
at dawn's bright aurora
and in the night, blue and pensive;
but one that invigorates everything, exalts, inflames,
pollen, sap, sinew, cortex, heat,
and gushes in torrents of life and leaps
from the breast of great Nature.

II

The Prince of Wales goes hunting
through woods and over mountains,
with his great retinue and with his hounds
of the most pedigree blood.

*

Hushing the throng of minions,
halting leashes and steeds,
with a restless gaze
he beholds the two tigers, at the grotto
entrance. He calls for the shotgun,
and advances, never wavering.

*

The beasts are caressing. They have taken no heed
of the hunting party.
Those terrible beings,
drunk on love-making,
with flowers and chains
might as well have been harnessed
to Cytherea's snowy conch
or Cupid's chariot.

*

The daring Prince
moves forward, closes in, has stopped;
has aimed with one eye shut; has fired;
the thunder of the shot
has echoed through the dense wood.
The male tiger runs away;
her belly torn open, the female stays.
Oh, she is dying! . . . But before, weak, stiffening,

chorreando sangre por la herida abierta,
con ojo dolorido
miró a aquel cazador; lanzó un gemido
como un ¡ay! de mujer . . . y cayó muerta.

III
Aquel macho que huyó, bravo y zahareño
a los rayos ardientes
del sol, en su cubil después dormía.
Entonces tuvo un sueño:
que enterraba las garras y los dientes
en vientres sonrosados
y pechos de mujer; y que engullía
por postres delicados
de comidas y cenas,—
como tigre goloso entre golosos,—
unas cuantas docenas
de niños tiernos, rubios y sabrosos.

AUTUMNAL

Eros, Vita, Lumen

En las pálidas tardes
yerran nubes tranquilas
en el azul; en las ardientes manos
se posan las cabezas pensativas.
¡Ah los suspiros! ¡Ah los dulces sueños!
¡Ah las tristezas íntimas!
¡Ah el polvo de oro que en el aire flota,
tras cuyas ondas trémulas se miran
los ojos tiernos y húmedos,
las bocas inundadas de sonrisas,
las crespas cabelleras
y los dedos de rosa que acarician!
*

En las pálidas tardes
me cuenta una hada amiga

as blood from the open wound flowed,
with a doleful eye
she looked at that hunter; she let out a moan
like a woman's cry . . . and falling, died.

III

That beast who, fierce and wild, ran away
in the burning rays
of the sun, later slept in his lair.
Then he had a dream:
he was burying his claws and teeth
in the pink bellies
and breasts of women; and for a dainty dessert
he was gobbling up
after every meal
—a gourmet tiger among gourmets—
several dozen
children, tender, blond, and savory.

IN AUTUMN

Eros, Vita, Lumen

In the pallid afternoons
clouds roam tranquil
in the blue; on their burning hands
they rest their pensive heads.
Ah, the sighs! Ah, the sweet dreams!
Ah, the intimate sorrows!
Ah, the gold dust floating in the air,
behind those tremulous waves
the damp and tender eyes exchange looks,
the mouths inundated with smiles,
the frizzy hair
and the caress of rosy fingers!
*
In the pallid afternoons
a friendly fairy tells me

las historias secretas
llenas de poesía;
lo que cantan los pájaros,
lo que llevan las brisas,
lo que vaga en las nieblas,
lo que sueñan las niñas.

*

Una vez sentí el ansia
de una sed infinita.
Dije al hada amorosa:
—Quiero en el alma mía
tener la inspiración honda, profunda,
inmensa: luz, calor, aroma, vida.
Ella me dijo:—¡Ven! con el acento
con que hablaría un arpa. En él había
un divino idioma de esperanza.
¡Oh sed del ideal!

*

Sobre la cima
de un monte, a medianoche,
me mostró las estrellas encendidas.
Era un jardín de oro
con pétalos de llama que titilan.
Exclamé:—Más . . .

*

La aurora
vino después. La aurora sonreía,
con la luz en la frente,
como la joven tímida
que abre la reja, y la sorprenden luego
ciertas curiosas, mágicas pupilas.
Y dije:—Más . . . Sonriendo
la celeste hada amiga
prorrumpió:—¡Y bien! ¡Las flores!

*

Y las flores
estaban frescas, lindas,
empapadas de olor: la rosa virgen,
la blanca margarita,

the secret stories
full of poetry;
which the birds sing,
which are carried on the breezes,
which wander in the mists,
which young girls dream.

*

Once I felt the pangs
of an infinite thirst.
I said to the amorous fairy:
"In my soul I want to sound
an inspiration deep, profound,
immense: light, aroma, life, heat."
She said: "Come!" in the tone
of a talking harp. It seemed
a divine idiom of hope.
O that thirst for the ideal!

*

     Above the top
of a mountain, at midnight,
she showed me the glowing stars.
It was a garden of gold
with twinkling petals of flame.
I cried out, "More . . ."

*

    The dawn
came after. The dawn was smiling,
with light on her brow,
like a shy young girl
who opens the lattice and is taken by surprise
by certain curious, magical eyes.
And I said, "More . . . " Smiling,
the friendly blue fairy
burst out: "As you wish! The flowers!"

*

    And the flowers
came up fresh, pretty,
soaked in scent: the virgin rose,
the white daisy,

la azucena gentil y las volúbiles
que cuelgan de la rama estremecida.
Y dije:—Más . . .

*

El viento
arrastraba rumores, ecos, risas,
murmullos misteriosos, aleteos,
músicas nunca oídas.
El hada entonces me llevó hasta el velo
que nos cubre las ansias infinitas,
la inspiración profunda,
y el alma de las liras.
Y lo rasgó. Y allí todo era aurora.
En el fondo se vía
un bello rostro de mujer.

*

¡Oh, nunca,
Piérides, diréis las sacras dichas
que en el alma sintiera!
Con su vaga sonrisa:—
—¿Más? . . . —dijo el hada.—Y yo tenía entonces,
clavadas las pupilas
en el azul; y en mis ardientes manos
se posó mi cabeza pensativa . . .

ANAGKE

Y dijo la paloma:
—Yo soy feliz. Bajo el inmenso cielo,
en el árbol en flor, junto a la poma
llena de miel, junto al retoño suave
y húmedo por las gotas de rocío,
tengo mi hogar. Y vuelo,
con mis anhelos de ave,
del amado árbol mío
hasta el bosque lejano,
cuando al himno jocundo
del despertar de Oriente,

the gentle Madonna lily and the convolvulus
that droops shivering from the bough.
And I said, "More . . . "
*

The wind
trailed murmurs, echoes, laughter,
mysterious whispers, the beating of wings,
kinds of music never heard before.
The fairy then carried me to the veil
that covers our infinite cravings,
the profound inspiration,
and the soul of the lyres.
And she rent it! And everything there was daybreak.
At its core appeared
a lovely female face.
*

Oh never,
Pierides, will you tell the sacred delights
which I felt in my soul!
With her vague smile:
"More? . . . ," said the fairy. And I had at the time
my pupils fastened
on the blue; and on my burning hands
I rested my pensive head . . .

ANAGKE

And said the dove:
"I am happy. Under the immense sky,
in the flowering tree, by the honey-filled
apple, next to the tender bud
watered by the dewdrops,
I have my home. And I fly,
with all the longing of a bird,
from this beloved tree of mine
to the distant forest,
when to the jocund anthem
of the waking of Orient,

sale el alba desnuda, y muestra al mundo
el pudor de la luz sobre su frente.
Mi ala es blanca y sedosa;
la luz la dora y baña
y céfiro la peina.
Son mis pies como pétalos de rosa.
Yo soy la dulce reina
que arrulla a su palomo en la montaña.
En el fondo del bosque pintoresco
está el alerce en que formé mi nido;
y tengo allí, bajo el follaje fresco,
un polluelo sin par, recién nacido.
Soy la promesa alada,
el juramento vivo;
soy quien lleva el recuerdo de la amada
para el enamorado pensativo;
yo soy la mensajera
de los tristes y ardientes soñadores,
que va a revolotear diciendo amores
junto a una perfumada cabellera.
Soy el lirio del viento.
Bajo el azul del hondo firmamento
muestro de mi tesoro bello y rico
las preseas y galas:
el arrullo en el pico,
la caricia en las alas.
Yo despierto a los pájaros parleros
y entonan sus melódicos cantares:
me poso en los floridos limoneros
y derramo una lluvia de azahares.
Yo soy toda inocente, toda pura.
Yo me esponjo en las ansias del deseo,
y me estremezco en la íntima ternura
de un roce, de un rumor, de un aleteo.
¡Oh, inmenso azul! Yo te amo. Porque a Flora
das la lluvia y el sol siempre encendido:
porque, siendo el palacio de la aurora,
también eres el techo de mi nido.
¡Oh, inmenso azul! Yo adoro

naked dawn arises, and shows to the world
the modesty of the light across her forehead.
My wing is white and silken;
the light bathes and gilds it
and a zephyr combs it.
My feet are like the petals of a rose.
I am the sweet queen
that coos to her dove on the mountain.
In the heart of the picturesque forest
stands the larch where I built my nest;
and I have there, under the cool foliage,
a chick without equal, newly born.
I am the winged promise,
the living oath;
the one who bears to the pensive lover
the memory of his sweetheart;
I am the messenger
of the sad and ardent dreamers,
hovering to speak love
near perfumed hair.
I am the lily of the wind.
Below the deep firmament's blue
I show of my rich and lovely treasure
its prizes and finery:
in the beak, a coo,
in the wings, a caress.
I awake the chattering birds
and they intone their melodic songs:
in the blooming lemon trees I perch
and pour a rain of lemon blossoms.
I am all innocent, all pure.
I bathe in the throes of desire,
and shiver in the intimate tenderness
of a glancing touch, of a murmur, of a flutter.
O immense blue! I love you. Because to Flora
you give the rain and the sun always aglow:
because, being the palace of dawn,
you are also the ceiling of my nest.
O immense blue! I adore

tus celajes risueños,
y esa niebla sutil de polvo de oro
donde van los perfumes y los sueños.
Amo los velos tenues, vagarosos,
de las flotantes brumas,
donde tiendo a los aires cariñosos
el sedeño abanico de mis plumas.
¡Soy feliz! porque es mía la floresta,
donde el misterio de los nidos se halla;
porque el alba es mi fiesta
y el amor mi ejercicio y mi batalla.
Feliz, porque de dulces ansias llena
calentar mis polluelos es mi orgullo,
porque en las selvas vírgenes resuena
la música celeste de mi arrullo,
porque no hay una rosa que no me ame,
ni pájaro gentil que no me escuche,
ni garrido cantor que no me llame.
—¿Sí?—dijo entonce un gavilán infame,
y con furor se la metió en el buche.
Entonces el buen Dios, allá en su trono,
(mientras Satán, para distraer su encono
aplaudía a aquel pájaro zahareño),
se puso a meditar. Arrugó el ceño,
y pensó, al recordar sus vastos planes,
y recorrer sus puntos y sus comas,
que cuando creó palomas
no debía haber creado gavilanes.

VENUS

En la tranquila noche, mis nostalgias amargas sufría.
En busca de quietud bajé al fresco y callado jardín.
En el obscuro cielo Venus bella temblando lucía,
como incrustado en ébano un dorado y divino jazmín.
A mi alma enamorada, una reina oriental parecía,
que esperaba a su amante, bajo el techo de su camarín,
o que, llevada en hombros, la profunda extensión recorría,

your smiling masses of cloud,
and that subtle mist of gold dust,
where dreams and perfumes walk.
I love the tenuous, roaming veils
of floating fogs,
where I extend to the affectionate breezes
the silken fan of my feathers.
I am happy! because the wood is mine,
where the mystery of nests is found;
because dawn is my festival
and love my exercise and battle.
Happy, because my pride is warming
my chicks with sweet full longing,
because in the virgin woods resounds
the celestial music of my cooing,
because there is no rose that I do not love,
nor gentle bird that does not hear me,
nor handsome singer that does not call me."
"Really?" said a wicked sparrow hawk,
savagely snapping her up in his craw.
Then the good Lord, up there on his throne
(while Satan, to distract his rancor,
was applauding that unruly bird),
began to ponder. His frown wrinkled
and he realized, recalling his vast plans,
and going over all his periods and commas,
that when he created doves
he should not have created hawks.

VENUS

I suffered bitter longings in the tranquil night.
I went to the cool and quiet garden seeking rest.
In deep dark heaven lovely Venus trembled brightly,
as a divine, gilded jasmine would in ebony nestle.
To my amorous soul, she seemed an Oriental queen
who, below the boudoir ceiling, awaited her lover,
or, carried aloft throughout her boundless realm by means

triunfante y luminosa, recostada sobre un palanquín.
"¡Oh, reina rubia!—díjele,—mi alma quiere dejar su crisálida
y volar hacia ti, y tus labios de fuego besar;
y flotar en el nimbo que derrama en tu frente luz pálida,
y en siderales éxtasis no dejarte un momento de amar."
El aire de la noche refrescaba la atmósfera cálida.
Venus, desde el abismo, me miraba con triste mirar.

WALT WHITMAN

En su país de hierro vive el gran viejo,
bello como un patriarca, sereno y santo.
Tiene en la arruga olímpica de su entrecejo,
algo que impera y vence con noble encanto.
Su alma del infinito parece espejo;
son sus cansados hombros dignos del manto;
y con arpa labrada de un roble añejo,
como un profeta nuevo canta su canto.
Sacerdote, que alienta soplo divino,
anuncia en el futuro, tiempo mejor.
Dice al águila: "¡Vuela!" "¡Boga!" al marino,
y "¡Trabaja!" al robusto trabajador.
¡Así va ese poeta por su camino
con su soberbio rostro de emperador!

SALVADOR DÍAZ MIRÓN

Tu cuarteto es cuadriga de águilas bravas
que aman las tempestades, los Oceanos;
las pesadas tizonas, las férreas clavas,
son las armas forjadas para tus manos.
Tu idea tiene cráteres y vierte lavas;
del Arte recorriendo montes y llanos,
van tus rudas estrofas jamás esclavas,
como un tropel de búfalos americanos.
Lo que suena en tu lira lejos resuena,
como cuando habla el bóreas, o cuando truena.

of bearers, lounged there luminous and triumphant above.
"O golden queen," I cried, "to float in the halo that spills
pale light upon your brow, my soul would shed its chrysalis
and fly away to you; and for you to love at will
in sidereal ecstasies, your fiery lips my soul would kiss."
Night refreshed the torrid atmosphere with a chill.
With her gaze of sadness Venus watched me from the abyss.

WALT WHITMAN

In his iron land lives an old man of renown,
comely as a patriarch, hallowed and assured.
Upon the Olympic furrow of his brow
he bears dominion and mastery of a noble allure.
His soul appears to mirror infinity;
worthy of a mantle are his weary shoulders;
and with a harp carved from age-old oak,
like some new prophet he sings his song.
This priest, who breathes a sigh divine,
announces in the future a better time:
"Soar!" he says to the eagle; to the sailor, "Sail!";
and "Work!" to the hearty laborer.
And so the poet makes his way
with the lofty look of an emperor!

SALVADOR DÍAZ MIRÓN

Your quatrain is a chariot drawn by wild
eagles that love the tempests and the oceans;
weighty Tizonas, ferrous bludgeons,
they are the arms forged by your hands.
Your idea holds craters and spews lava;
your stanzas, rude and never enslaved, roam
over plains and mountains of Art
like vast herds of American buffalo.
The sound from your lyre resounds afar,
as when Boreas speaks or when it thunders.

¡Hijo del Nuevo Mundo! la humanidad
oiga, sobre la frente de las naciones,
la hímnica pompa lírica de tus canciones
que saludan triunfantes la Libertad.

Child of the New World! may all mankind
hear, upon the face of the nations,
the lyrical, hymnical pomp of your songs
triumphantly saluting Liberty.

Ruben Dario.

Canto a la Argentina y otros Poemas.

Biblioteca Corona. *Madrid 1914.*

Darío's last book of poetry, published in Madrid in 1914, two years before his death. Between 1914 and 1916 this same Spanish publishing house produced Darío's personal selection of his own poetry, *Obra poética,* which spanned three volumes and which has been edited under the title *Y una sed de ilusiones infinita.*

A Carlos Vega Belgrano afectuosamente
este libro dedica R.D.

PALABRAS LIMINARES

Después de *Azul* . . . después de *Los Raros*, voces insinuantes, buena y mala intención, entusiasmo sonoro y envidia subterránea,—todo bella cosecha—solicitaron lo que, en conciencia, no he creído fructuoso ni oportuno: un manifiesto.

Ni fructuoso ni oportuno:

a) Por la absoluta falta de elevación mental de la mayoría pensante de nuestro continente, en la cual impera el universal personaje clasificado por Remy de Gourmont con el nombre de Celui-qui-ne-comprend-pas. Celui-qui-ne-comprend-pas es entre nosotros profesor, académico correspondiente de la Real Academia Española, periodista, abogado, poeta, rastaquouer;

b) Porque la obra colectiva de los nuevos de América es aún vana, estando muchos de los mejores talentos en el limbo de un completo desconocimiento del mismo Arte a que se consagran;

c) Porque proclamando como proclamo, una estética acrática, la imposición de un modelo o de un código, implicaría una contradicción.

Yo no tengo literatura «mía»—como lo ha manifestado una magistral autoridad,—para marcar el rumbo de los demás: mi literatura es *mía* en mí;—quien siga servilmente mis huellas perderá su tesoro personal y, paje o esclavo, no podrá ocultar sello o librea. Wagner a Augusta Holmes, su discípula, dijo un día: «lo primero, no imitar a nadie, y sobre todo, a mí». Gran decir.

***

Yo he dicho, en la misa rosa de mi juventud, mis antífonas, mis secuencias, mis profanas prosas. Tiempo y menos fatigas de alma y corazón me han hecho falta, para, como un buen monje artífice, hacer mis mayúsculas dignas de cada página del breviario. (A través de los fuegos divinos de las vidrieras historiadas, me río del viento que sopla afuera, del mal que pasa.) Tocad, campanas de oro, campanas de plata, tocad todos los días llamándome a la fiesta en que brillan los ojos de fuego, y las rosas de las bocas sangran delicias únicas. Mi órgano es un viejo clavicordio pompadour, al son del

PROFANE PROSE AND OTHER POEMS
(1896, 1901)

To Carlos Vega Belgrano, affectionately,
this book is dedicated by R.D.

LIMINARY WORDS

After *Azul* . . . , after *Los raros* [*The Eccentrics*], insinuating voices, good
will and spite, resounding enthusiasm and subterranean envy,—an altogether
handsome harvest—requested what I, in good conscience, have thought
neither fruitful nor appropriate: a manifesto.

Neither fruitful nor appropriate:

a) For the absolute lack of mental elevation in the thinking majority on
our continent, where a universal public figure, whom Remy de Gourmont
has classified by the name *Celui-qui-ne-comprend-pas*, holds sway. *Celui-qui-
ne-comprend-pas* is, among us, a professor, an academic corresponding mem-
ber of the Spanish Royal Academy, a journalist, a lawyer, a poet, a parvenu;

b) Because the collective work of the new Americans is still vain, many
of the best talents existing in a limbo of complete ignorance of the very Art
to which they consecrate themselves;

c) Because by proclaiming what I proclaim—an anarchic esthetic—,
the imposition of a model or code would entail a contradiction.

I have no literature that is "mine"—as one overbearing authority has
put it—, in order to blaze a trail for the rest; my literature is *mine* in me;
whoever obsequiously follows in my footsteps will lose his personal treasure
and, page or slave, will be unable to hide the hallmark or livery. Wagner to
Augusta Holmes, his disciple, said one day: "First of all, imitate no one, and
least of all me." A worthy saying.

***

I have spoken, in the pink Mass of my youth, my antiphons, my se-
quences, my profane prose. I have required time and less weariness of heart
and soul in order to make, like a good craftsman monk, my capital letters
worthy of each page in the breviary. (Through the divine fires of the leaded,
historiated windows, I laugh at the wind blowing outside, at the evil passing
by.) Chime on, golden bells, silver bells, chime every day, calling me to the
festival where fiery eyes shine, and the roses of their mouths bleed unique
delights. My organ is an old Pompadour clavichord, at the sound of which

111

cual danzaron sus gavotas alegres abuelos; y el perfume de tu pecho es mi perfume, eterno incensario de carne, Varona inmortal, flor de mi costilla.

Hombre soy.

***

¿Hay en mi sangre alguna gota de sangre de Africa, o de indio chorotega o nagrandano? Pudiera ser, a despecho de mis manos de marqués: mas he aquí que veréis en mis versos princesas, reyes, cosas imperiales, visiones de países lejanos o imposibles: qué queréis! yo detesto la vida y el tiempo en que me tocó nacer; y a un presidente de República no podré saludarle en el idioma en que te cantaría a ti, oh Halagabal! de cuya corte—oro, seda, mármol—me acuerdo en sueños . . .

(Si hay poesía en nuestra América ella está en las cosas viejas, en Palenke y Utatlán, en el indio legendario, y en el inca sensual y fino, y en el gran Moctezuma de la silla de oro. Lo demás es tuyo, demócrata Walt Whitman.)

Buenos Aires: Cosmópolis.

Y mañana!

***

El abuelo español de barba blanca me señala una serie de retratos ilustres: «Este, me dice, es el gran don Miguel de Cervantes Saavedra, genio y manco; este es Lope de Vega, este Garcilaso, este Quintana.» Yo le pregunto por el noble Gracián, por Teresa la Santa, por el bravo Góngora y el más fuerte de todos, don Francisco de Quevedo y Villegas. Después exclamo: Shakespeare! Dante! Hugo! . . . (Y en mi interior: Verlaine . . .!)

Luego, al despedirme:—«Abuelo, preciso es decíroslo: mi esposa es de mi tierra; mi querida, de París.»

***

Y la cuestión métrica? Y el ritmo?

Como cada palabra tiene una alma, hay en cada verso, además de la armonía verbal, una melodía ideal. La música es sólo de la idea, muchas veces.

***

La gritería de trescientas ocas no te impedirá, silvano, tocar tu encantadora flauta, con tal de que tu amigo el ruiseñor, esté contento de tu melodía. Cuando él no esté para escucharte, cierra los ojos y toca para los habitantes de tu reino interior. ¡Oh pueblo de desnudas ninfas, de rosadas reinas, de amorosas diosas!

Cae a tus pies una rosa, otra rosa, otra rosa. Y besos!

***

happy grandfathers danced their gavottes; and the perfume of your breast is my perfume, an eternal censer of flesh, immortal Varona, flower of my rib.

I am a man.

***

Is there in my blood a drop of blood from Africa or of Chorotega or Nagrandan Indian? It may well be, despite my hands of a Marquis: yet note here that you will see in my verses princesses, kings, imperial matters, visions of lands remote or impossible: what do you expect? I detest the life and times into which I had to be born; and I will be unable to greet a president of the Republic in the language in which I would sing to you, O Elagabalus! whose court—gold, silk, marble—I recall in dreams . . .

(If there is poetry in our America, it is in the old things, in Palenque and Utatlan, in the legendary Indian, and in the courtly and sensual Inca, and in the great Montezuma on the golden seat. The rest is yours, democratic Walt Whitman.)

Buenos Aires: Cosmopolis.

And tomorrow!

***

My white-whiskered Spanish grandfather points out to me a series of illustrious portraits: "This one," he tells me, "is the great Don Miguel de Cervantes Saavedra, a one-armed genius; this one is Lope de Vega, this one Garcilaso, this one Quintana." I ask him about the noble Gracián, about Theresa the Saint, about the courageous Góngora and the strongest of all, Don Francisco de Quevedo y Villegas. Then I exclaim: Shakespeare! Dante! Hugo! . . . (And in my heart: Verlaine . . . !)

Later, when saying good-bye: "Grandfather, I have to tell you: the woman I married is from my native land: the woman I love, from Paris."

***

And the question of meter? And rhythm?

Since each word has a soul, there is in each verse, in addition to the verbal harmony, an ideal melody. The music is made only from the idea, quite often.

***

The hissing of three hundred geese will not stop you, sylvan, from playing your enchanted flute, provided that your friend the nightingale is happy with your tune. When he is not there to listen, close your eyes and play for the inhabitants of your inner realm. O nation of naked nymphs, of pink queens, of amorous goddesses!

A rose will fall at your feet, then another and another. And kisses!

***

Y, la primera ley, creador: crear. Bufe el eunuco; cuando una musa te dé un hijo, queden las otras ocho en cinta.

R. D.

ERA UN AIRE SUAVE . . .

Era un aire suave, de pausados giros;
el hada Harmonía ritmaba sus vuelos;
e iban frases vagas y tenues suspiros
entre los sollozos de los violoncelos.

Sobre la terraza, junto a los ramajes,
diríase un trémolo de liras eolias
cuando acariciaban los sedosos trajes
sobre el tallo erguidas las blancas magnolias.

La marquesa Eulalia risas y desvíos
daba a un tiempo mismo para dos rivales,
el vizconde rubio de los desafíos
y el abate joven de los madrigales.

Cerca, coronado con hojas de viña,
reía en su máscara Término barbudo,
y, como un efebo que fuese una niña,
mostraba una Diana su mármol desnudo.

Y bajo un boscaje del amor palestra,
sobre rico zócalo al modo de Jonia,
con un candelabro prendido en la diestra
volaba el Mercurio de Juan de Bolonia.

La orquesta perlaba sus mágicas notas,
un coro de sones alados se oía;
galantes pavanas, fugaces gavotas
cantaban los dulces violines de Hungría.

Al oír las quejas de sus caballeros
ríe, ríe, ríe, la divina Eulalia,

And, the first rule, creator: create. Let the eunuch bray; when one of the muses gives you a son, may the other eight be pregnant.

R.D.

IT WAS A GENTLE AIR . . .

It was a gentle air, with leisurely turns;
the fairy Harmony lent rhythm to its flights;
and vague phrases and tenuous sighs would slip
between the sobs of the violoncellos.

On the terrace, alongside the branches,
what might be called a tremolo of Aeolian lyres
when the silken costumes caressed
white magnolias upright on the stem.

The Marquise Eulalia laughter and snub
bestowed at the same time upon two rivals,
the blond viscount of duels
and the young abbot of madrigals.

Nearby, crowned with leaves from the vineyard,
bearded Terminus was laughing into his mask,
and, like some ephebe who might be a girl,
a Diana showed off her naked marble.

And under a grove in the arena of love,
on a tasteful socle in the Ionic style,
with a lighted candelabra in his right hand
Giovanni da Bologna's Mercury was in flight.

The orchestra pearled its magical notes,
a chorus of winged sounds was heard;
the sweet violins of Hungary sang
courtly pavans, fleeting gavottes.

Hearing complaints from her gentlemen
the divine Eulalia laughs, and laughs, and laughs,

pues son su tesoro las flechas de Eros,
el cinto de Cipria, la rueca de Onfalia.

¡Ay de quien sus mieles y frases recoja!
¡Ay de quien del canto de su amor se fíe!
Con sus ojos lindos y su boca roja,
la divina Eulalia, ríe, ríe, ríe.

Tiene azules ojos, es maligna y bella;
cuando mira vierte viva luz extraña:
se asoma a sus húmedas pupilas de estrella
el alma del rubio cristal de Champaña.

Es noche de fiesta, y el baile de trajes
ostenta su gloria de triunfos mundanos.
La divina Eulalia, vestida de encajes,
una flor destroza con sus tersas manos.

El teclado armónico de su risa fina
a la alegre música de un pájaro iguala,
con los staccati de una bailarina
y las locas fugas de una colegiala.

¡Amoroso pájaro que trinos exhala
bajo el ala a veces ocultando el pico;
que desdenes rudos lanza bajo el ala,
bajo el ala aleve del leve abanico!

Cuando a medianoche sus notas arranque
y en arpegios áureos gima Filomela,
y el ebúrneo cisne, sobre el quieto estanque
como blanca góndola imprima su estela,

la marquesa alegre llegará al boscaje,
boscaje que cubre la amable glorieta
donde han de estrecharla los brazos de un paje,
que siendo su paje será su poeta.

as her treasure consists of Eros's arrows,
the Cyprian's sash, and Omphale's distaff.

Alas for him who gathers her honey and phrases!
Alas for him who relies on the song of her love!
With her delightful eyes and her red mouth
the divine Eulalia laughs, and laughs, and laughs.

She has blue eyes, is malicious and lovely;
when she looks, she spills a bright strange light;
peeping from her starry moist eyes
is the soul of the golden crystal of Champaign.

It is a festive night, and the costume ball
flaunts its glory of mundane triumphs.
The divine Eulalia, dressed in lace,
shreds a flower in her smooth hands.

The harmonic keyboard of her fine laughter
equates to the happy music of a bird,
with the *staccati* of a ballerina
and the mad flights of a schoolgirl.

Amorous bird exhaling trills
beneath its wing, sometimes hiding its beak,
tossing off rude mockeries beneath its wing,
beneath the treacherous wing of a small, slight fan!

When at midnight Philomela moans
in golden arpeggios and drags out her notes,
and the eburnean swan, on the quiet pond,
prints its wake like a white gondola,

The gay Marquise will arrive at the grove,
a grove that covers the pleasant arbor
where a page will take her in his arms,
who, being her page, must be her poet.

Al compás de un canto de artista de Italia
que en la brisa errante la orquesta deslíe,
junto a los rivales la divina Eulalia,
la divina Eulalia, ríe, ríe, ríe.

¿Fue acaso en el tiempo del rey Luis de Francia,
sol con corte de astros, en campos de azur?
¿Cuando los alcázares llenó de fragancia
la regia y pomposa rosa Pompadour?

¿Fue cuando la bella su falda cogía
con dedos de ninfa, bailando el minué,
y de los compases el ritmo seguía
sobre el tacón rojo, lindo y leve el pie?

¿O cuando pastoras de floridos valles
ornaban con cintas sus albos corderos,
y oían, divinas Tirsis de Versalles,
las declaraciones de sus caballeros?

¿Fue en ese buen tiempo de duques pastores,
de amantes princesas y tiernos galanes,
cuando entre sonrisas y perlas y flores
iban las casacas de los chambelanes?

¿Fue acaso en el Norte o en el Mediodía?
Yo el tiempo y el día y el país ignoro,
pero sé que Eulalia ríe todavía,
¡y es cruel y eterna su risa de oro!

SONATINA

La princesa está triste . . . ¿qué tendrá la princesa?
Los suspiros se escapan de su boca de fresa,
que ha perdido la risa, que ha perdido el color.
La princesa está pálida en su silla de oro,
está mudo el teclado de su clave sonoro;
y en un vaso olvidada se desmaya una flor.

In time with a song by an Italian artist
which the orchestra unravels in the meandering breeze,
beside the rivals the divine Eulalia,
the divine Eulalia laughs, and laughs, and laughs.

Was it perhaps in the time of King Louis of France,
a sun with a court of stars in fields of azure?
When Pompadour, the regal and pompous rose,
filled the palaces with fragrance?

Was it when a beauty would lift her skirts
with the fingers of a nymph, dancing the minuet,
and her light and lovely foot would follow
the rhythm of the beats on a red heel?

Or when shepherdesses in flowered valleys
adorned their snow-white lambs with ribbons,
and heard, divine Thyrsis of Versailles,
the declarations of their gentlemen?

Was it in that fair time of shepherd-dukes,
of princess-lovers and tender suitors,
when among smiles and pearls and flowers
the doublets of the chamberlains would pass?

Was it perhaps in the North or in the Noon?
Neither age nor day nor land do I know,
only that Eulalia still is laughing,
and cruel and eternal is her laugh of gold!

SONATINA

The princess is sad . . . What is wrong with the princess?
Her sighs are escaping from her strawberry mouth,
which has lost all its laughter, which has lost all its color.
The princess is pale on her golden divan,
the keyboard is mute on her resonant harpsichord;
and a flower, forgotten, has swooned in a vase.

El jardín puebla el triunfo de los pavos-reales.
Parlanchina, la dueña dice cosas banales,
y, vestido de rojo piruetea el bufón.
La princesa no ríe, la princesa no siente;
la princesa persigue por el cielo de Oriente
la libélula vaga de una vaga ilusión.

¿Piensa acaso en el príncipe de Golconda o de China,
o en el que ha detenido su carroza argentina
para ver de sus ojos la dulzura de luz?
O en el rey de las Islas de las Rosas fragantes,
o en el que es soberano de los claros diamantes,
o en el dueño orgulloso de las perlas de Ormuz?

¡Ay! la pobre princesa de la boca de rosa,
quiere ser golondrina, quiere ser mariposa,
tener alas ligeras, bajo el cielo volar,
ir al sol por la escala luminosa de un rayo,
saludar a los lirios con los versos de Mayo,
o perderse en el viento sobre el trueno del mar.

Ya no quiere el palacio, ni la rueca de plata,
ni el halcón encantado, ni el bufón escarlata,
ni los cisnes unánimes en el lago de azur.
Y están tristes las flores por la flor de la corte;
los jazmines de Oriente, los nelumbos del Norte,
de Occidente las dalias y las rosas del Sur.

¡Pobrecita princesa de los ojos azules!
Está presa en sus oros, está presa en sus tules,
en la jaula de mármol del palacio real;
el palacio soberbio que vigilan los guardas,
que custodian cien negros con sus cien alabardas,
un lebrel que no duerme y un dragón colosal.

¡Oh quién fuera hipsipila que dejó la crisálida!
(La princesa está triste. La princesa está pálida)
¡Oh visión adorada de oro, rosa y marfil!
¡Quién volara a la tierra donde un príncipe existe

A triumph of peacocks has peopled the garden.
Loquacious, the chaperone talks of banalities,
and the jester, in red, is performing his tricks.
The princess won't laugh, no, the princess feels nothing;
the princess pursues on the sky of the East
the nebulous dragonfly of a nebulous dream.

Is she thinking perhaps of the prince of Golconda or China,
or the one who has stopped his argentine coach
just to look at the sweetness of light in her eyes?
Or the king of the fragrant Islands of Roses,
or the one who is sovereign of diamonds so clear,
or the haughty possessor of the pearls of Hormuz?

Alas! The poor princess with the rose-colored mouth
would rather a swallow or a butterfly be,
and under the heavens would fly on light wings,
would rise to the sun on the luminous ladder of beams,
would greet every lily with the verses of May,
or be lost in the wind on the boom of the sea.

She no longer cares for the palace, nor the distaff of silver,
nor the spellbound falcon, nor the scarlet buffoon,
nor unanimous swans in the azure lagoon.
And the flowers are sad for the flower at court:
from the Orient, jasmines; and nelumbos from the North;
from the West there are dahlias, and the rose from the South.

The poor little princess with her eyes of blue!
She's imprisoned in gold, she's imprisoned in tulle,
within the marble cage of the royal palace;
the superb royal palace where the guards hold their watch,
a hundred black men with a hundred tall halberds,
a vigilant hound and gargantuan dragon.

Oh to be a hypsipyle that sheds its cocoon!
(The princess is sad. The princess is pale.)
Oh adorable vision of gold, of roses and ivory!
To fly to the land where a prince does exist

(La princesa está pálida. La princesa está triste)
más brillante que el alba, más hermoso que Abril!

Calla, calla, princesa, —dice el hada madrina—
en caballo con alas, hacia acá se encamina,
en el cinto la espada y en la mano el azor,
el feliz caballero que te adora sin verte,
y que llega de lejos, vencedor de la Muerte,
a encenderte los labios con su beso de amor!

ITE, MISSA EST

A Reynaldo de Rafael

Yo adoro a una sonámbula con alma de Eloísa
virgen como la nieve y honda como la mar;
su espíritu es la hostia de mi amorosa misa
y alzo al son de una dulce lira crepuscular.

Ojos de evocadora, gesto de profetisa,
en ella hay la sagrada frecuencia del altar;
su risa es la sonrisa suave de Monna Lisa,
sus labios son los únicos labios para besar.

Y he de besarla un día con rojo beso ardiente;
apoyada en mi brazo como convaleciente
me mirará asombrada con íntimo pavor;

la enamorada esfinge quedará estupefacta,
apagaré la llama de la vestal intacta
y la faunesa antigua me rugirá de amor!

COLOQUIO DE LOS CENTAUROS

A Paul Groussac.

En la isla en que detiene su esquife el argonauta
del inmortal Ensueño, donde la eterna pauta

(The princess is pale. The princess is sad.)
more dazzling than dawn, more handsome than April!

"Hush now, hush now, princess," says the fairy godmother,
"on a horse with great wings, he is coming for you,
with a sword in his belt and a hawk on his arm,
the goodly knight who adores you unseen,
and who comes from afar, having overcome Death,
to light up your lips with his kiss of true love."

ITE, MISSA EST

For Reynaldo de Rafael

I adore a sleepwalker with Héloïse's soul,
virgin as the snow and deep as the sea;
her spirit is the Host of my amorous Mass
and I rise to the beat of a sweet crepuscular lyre.

Eyes of an enchantress, the look of a prophetess,
there is in her the altar's sacred frequency;
her laugh is the soft smile of the Mona Lisa,
her lips are the only lips to kiss.

And I will kiss her one day with a red-hot kiss;
propped on my arm like a convalescent
she will gaze at me bewildered with intimate fright;

the enamored sphinx will be amazed,
I will quench the flame of the intact vestal virgin
and the lady faun of antiquity will roar at me for love!

COLLOQUY OF THE CENTAURS

For Paul Groussac

On the island where the Argonaut of immortal Fantasy
stopped his skiff, where the eternal standard

de las eternas liras se escucha:—Isla de Oro
en que el tritón elige su caracol sonoro
y la sirena blanca va a ver el sol—un día
se oye un tropel vibrante de fuerza y de armonía.

Son los Centauros. Cubren la llanura. Les siente
la montaña. De lejos, forman son de torrente
que cae; su galope al aire que reposa
despierta, y estremece la hoja del laurel-rosa.

Son los Centauros. Unos enormes, rudos; otros
alegres y saltantes como jóvenes potros;
unos con largas barbas como los padres-ríos,
otros imberbes, ágiles y de piafantes bríos,
y de robustos músculos, brazos y lomos aptos
para portar las ninfas rosadas en los raptos.

Van en galope rítmico. Junto a un fresco boscaje,
frente al gran Oceano, se paran. El paisaje
recibe de la urna matinal luz sagrada
que el vasto azul suaviza con límpida mirada.
Y oyen seres terrestres y habitantes marinos
la voz de los crinados cuadrúpedos divinos.

QUIRÓN
Calladas las bocinas a los tritones gratas,
calladas las sirenas de labios escarlatas,
los carrillos de Eolo desinflados, digamos
junto al laurel ilustre de florecidos ramos
la gloria inmarcesible de las Musas hermosas
y el triunfo del terrible misterio de las cosas.
He aquí que renacen los lauros milenarios;
vuelven a dar su lumbre los viejos lampadarios;
y anímase en mi cuerpo de Centauro inmortal
la sangre del celeste caballo paternal.

RETO
Arquero luminoso, desde el zodíaco llegas;
aun presas en las crines tienes abejas griegas;

for the eternal lyres is heard—the Golden Isle
where the triton chooses his sonorous shell
and the white mermaid goes to see the sun—one day
a throng, vibrant with force and harmony, is heard.

They are the Centaurs. They cover the plain. The mountain
senses them. From afar they form the sound of a torrent
falling; their gallop wakes the air
from its repose and shakes the leaf of the rosebay.

They are the Centaurs. Some enormous, gruff; others
merry and skipping like young colts;
some with long beards like father rivers,
others beardless, agile and vigorous of hoof,
and with sturdy muscles, arms and backs fit
for carrying off pink nymphs in their abductions.

They move at a rhythmic gallop. Beside a cool grove,
facing the great Ocean, they halt. The landscape
receives sacred light from the morning urn
which the vast blue softens with a limpid glance.
And terrestrial beings and maritime denizens hear
the voice of the maned divine quadrupeds.

CHIRON

Now that the horns so pleasing to the tritons are hushed,
now that the mermaids with scarlet lips are hushed,
and the cheeks of Aeolus deflated, let us tell
by the illustrious laurel with flowering branches
the unfading glory of the lovely Muses
and the triumph of the terrible mystery of things.
Behold, the millennial laurels are reborn;
once again the old lampadaries give their glow;
and in my immortal Centaur body
the blood of the heavenly paternal horse is stirring.

RHOETUS

Luminous archer, from the Zodiac you come;
still imprisoned in your mane you have Greek bees;

aún del dardo herakleo muestras la roja herida
por do salir no pudo la esencia de tu vida.
Padre y Maestro excelso! Eres la fuente sana
de la verdad que busca la triste raza humana:
aun Esculapio sigue la vena de tu ciencia;
siempre el veloz Aquiles sustenta su existencia
con el manjar salvaje que le ofreciste un día,
y Herakles, descuidando su maza, en la armonía
de los astros, se eleva bajo el cielo nocturno . . .

QUIRÓN
La ciencia es flor del tiempo: mi padre fue Saturno.

ABANTES
Himnos a la sagrada Naturaleza; al vientre
de la tierra y al germen que entre las rocas y entre
las carnes de los árboles, y dentro humana forma
es un mismo secreto y es una misma norma,
potente y sutilísimo, universal resumen
de la suprema fuerza, de la virtud del Numen.

QUIRÓN
Himnos! Las cosas tienen un ser vital: las cosas
tienen raros aspectos, miradas misteriosas;
toda forma es un gesto, una cifra, un enigma;
en cada átomo existe un incógnito estigma;
cada hoja de cada árbol canta un propio cantar
y hay una alma en cada una de las gotas del mar;
el vate, el sacerdote, suele oír el acento
desconocido; a veces enuncia el vago viento
un misterio; y revela una inicial la espuma
o la flor; y se escuchan palabras de la bruma.
Y el hombre favorito del numen, en la linfa
o la ráfaga, encuentra mentor;—demonio o ninfa.

FOLO
El biforme ixionida comprende de la altura,
por la materna gracia, la lumbre que fulgura,
la nube que se anima de luz y que decora

still from the Herculean shaft you show the red wound
through which the essence of your life could not leave.
Father and Master sublime! You are the healing source
of the truth which the sad human race is seeking:
still Aesculapius follows the vein of your science;
swift Achilles always sustained his existence
with the savage delicacy which you offered him one day,
and Heracles, disregarding his club, in the harmony
of the stars, rose up beneath the nocturnal sky . . .

CHIRON

Science is a flower of time: my father was Saturn.

ABANTES

Hymns to sacred Nature; to the womb
of the earth and to the germ that, among rocks and among
the flesh of the trees and within the human form,
is a secret and a norm at the same time,
potent and exceedingly subtle, a universal summary
of the supreme power, the virtue of the Numen.

CHIRON

Hymns! Things have a vital being: things
have rare aspects, mysterious gazes;
each form is a gesture, a cipher, an enigma;
in each atom a stigma exists incognito;
every leaf of every tree sings its own song
and there is a soul in each and every drop of the sea;
the bard, the priest, is accustomed to hear the unknown
accent; sometimes the vague wind enunciates
a mystery; and an initial is revealed by the foam
or the flower; and one listens to words in the fog.
And the numen's chosen man, in the lymph
or the gust, finds a mentor: fiend or nymph.

PHOLUS

The dual-form Ixionid understands from on high,
because of his maternal grace, the brilliance that shines,
the cloud that brightens with light and decorates

el pavimento en donde rige su carro Aurora,
y la banda de Iris que tiene siete rayos
cual la lira en sus brazos siete cuerdas; los mayos
en la fragante tierra llenos de ramos bellos,
y el Polo coronado de cándidos cabellos.
El ixionida pasa veloz por la montaña
rompiendo con el pecho de la maleza huraña
los erizados brazos, las cárceles hostiles;
escuchan sus orejas los ecos más sutiles:
sus ojos atraviesan las intrincadas hojas
mientras sus manos toman para sus bocas rojas
las frescas bayas altas que el sátiro codicia;
junto a la oculta fuente su mirada acaricia
las curvas de las ninfas del séquito de Diana;
pues en su cuerpo corre también la esencia humana
unida a la corriente de la savia divina
y a la salvaje sangre que hay en la bestia equina.
Tal el hijo robusto de Ixión y de la Nube.

QUIRÓN
Sus cuatro patas, bajan; su testa erguida, sube.

ORNEO
Yo comprendo el secreto de la bestia. Malignos
seres hay y benignos. Entre ellos se hacen signos
de bien y mal, de odio o de amor, o de pena
o gozo: el cuervo es malo y la torcaz es buena.

QUIRÓN
Ni es la torcaz benigna, ni es el cuervo protervo:
son formas del Enigma la paloma y el cuervo.

ASTILO
El Enigma es el soplo que hace cantar la lira.

NESO
El Enigma es el rostro fatal de Deyanira!
Mi espalda aún guarda el dulce perfume de la bella;
aún mis pupilas llama su claridad de estrella.

the pavement where Aurora steers her cart,
and the band of Iris which has seven rays
as the lyre in her arms, seven strings; the Mays
on this fragrant earth, full of beautiful bouquets,
and the Pole crowned by white tresses.
The Ixionid passes quickly over the mountain
breaking with his chest the prickly arms
of the surly underbrush, hostile jails;
his ears heed the most subtle echoes:
his eyes pierce the intricate leaves
while his hands pluck for his red jaws
the high fresh berries that the satyr covets;
beside the hidden spring his gaze caresses
the curves of the nymphs in Diana's retinue;
in his body the human essence also runs,
united to the current of the divine sap
and to the savage blood that exists in the equine beast.
Such is the hardy son of Ixion and the Cloud.

CHIRON

His four feet, they go down; his erect head, it goes up.

ORNEUS

I understand the secret of the beast. Malevolent
beings exist, and benevolent. Among them are signs
of good and evil, of hate or of love, either pain
or pleasure: the crow is evil and the dove is good.

CHIRON

Neither is the dove benign, nor the crow ignoble:
they are forms of the Enigma, the dove and the crow.

ASTYLUS

The Enigma is the breath that makes the lyre sing.

NESSUS

The Enigma is the fatal face of Deianira!
My back still retains the beauty's sweet perfume;
still my pupils summon her star-like clarity.

¡Oh aroma de su sexo! ¡oh rosas y alabastros!
¡Oh envidias de las flores y celos de los astros!

QUIRÓN
Cuando del sacro abuelo la sangre luminosa
con la marina espuma formara nieve y rosa,
hecha de rosa y nieve nació la Anadiomena.
Al cielo alzó los brazos la lírica sirena,
los curvos hipocampos sobre las verdes ondas
levaron los hocicos; y caderas redondas,
tritónicas melenas y dorsos de delfines
junto a la Reina nueva se vieron. Los confines
del mar llenó el grandioso clamor; el universo
sintió que un nombre armónico, sonoro como un verso
llenaba el hondo hueco de la altura; ese nombre
hizo gemir la tierra de amor: fue para el hombre
más alto que el de Jove: y los númenes mismos
lo oyeron asombrados; los lóbregos abismos
tuvieron una gracia de luz. ¡VENUS impera!
Ella es entre las reinas celestes la primera,
pues es quien tiene el fuerte poder de la Hermosura.
Vaso de miel y mirra brotó de la amargura!
Ella es la más gallarda de las emperatrices;
princesa de los gérmenes, reina de las matrices,
señora de las savias y de las atracciones,
señora de los besos y de los corazones.

EURITO
No olvidaré los ojos radiantes de Hipodamia!

HIPEA
Yo sé de la hembra humana la original infamia.
Venus anima artera sus máquinas fatales,
tras los radiantes ojos ríen traidores males,
de su floral perfume se exhala sutil daño;
su cráneo obscuro alberga bestialidad y engaño.
Tiene las formas puras del ánfora, y la risa
del agua que la brisa riza y el sol irisa;
mas la ponzoña ingénita su máscara pregona:

O the aroma of her sex! O the roses and alabaster!
O the envies of the flowers and the jealousies of the stars!

CHIRON

When the holy grandfather's luminous blood
with the sea foam formed snow and rose,
of rose and snow was born Anadyomene.
The lyrical mermaid raised her arms to the sky,
the curved sea horses over the green waves
lifted their muzzles; and rounded haunches,
tritonic manes and dolphin humps
were seen beside the new Queen. The magnificent clamor
filled the confines of the sea; the universe
felt that a harmonic name, sonorous as a verse,
was filling the great hole of the deep. That name
made the earth groan for love: it was, for man,
higher than that of Jove: and the numina themselves,
astounded, heard it; the gloomy abysses
received a grace of light. VENUS reigns!
She is, among the heavenly queens, the first,
since it is she who has the mighty power of Beauty.
A cup of honey and myrrh sprang from bitterness!
She is the most graceful of the empresses;
princess of origins, queen of wombs,
lady of the lifeblood and of attractions,
lady of kisses and of hearts.

EURYTUS

I will not forget the radiant eyes of Hippodamia!

HYPEAS

I know the human female's original infamy.
Crafty Venus animates her fatal machines,
behind those radiant eyes treacherous evils laugh,
on her floral perfume a subtle harm is exhaled;
her dark cranium houses bestiality and deceit.
She has the pure forms of an amphora, and the laughter
of water which the breeze ripples and the sun makes iridescent;
yet the inborn poison reveals her mask:

mejores son el águila, la yegua y la leona.
De su húmeda impureza brota el calor que enerva
los mismos sacros dones de la imperial Minerva;
y entre sus duros pechos, lirios del Aqueronte,
hay un olor que llena la barca de Caronte.

ODITES

Como una miel celeste hay en su lengua fina;
su piel de flor aún húmeda está de agua marina.
Yo he visto de Hipodamia la faz encantadora,
la cabellera espesa, la pierna vencedora.
Ella de la hembra humana fuera ejemplar augusto;
ante su rostro olímpico no habría rostro adusto;
las Gracias junto a ella quedarían confusas,
y las ligeras Horas y las sublimes Musas
por ella detuvieran sus giros y su canto.

HIPEA

Ella la causa fuera de inenarrable espanto:
por ella el ixionida dobló su cuello fuerte.
La hembra humana es hermana del Dolor y la Muerte.

QUIRÓN

Por suma ley un día llegará el himeneo
que el soñador aguarda: Cinis será Ceneo;
claro será el origen del femenino arcano:
la Esfinge tal secreto dirá a su soberano.

CLITO

Naturaleza tiende sus brazos y sus pechos
a los humanos seres; la clave de los hechos
conócela el vidente; Homero con su báculo,
en su gruta Deifobe, la lengua del Oráculo.

CAUMANTES

El monstruo expresa un ansia del corazón del Orbe,
en el Centauro el bruto la vida humana absorbe,
el sátiro es la selva sagrada y la lujuria,
une sexuales ímpetus a la armoniosa furia.

better are the eagle, the mare, and the lioness.
From her damp impurity springs the heat that unnerves
even the sacred gifts of imperial Minerva;
and between her hard breasts, lilies of Acheron,
there is an odor that fills Charon's boat.

ODITES

There is something like celestial honey on her sharp tongue;
her flower-like skin is still moist from aquamarine.
I have seen Hippodamia's enchanting countenance,
the thick hair, the triumphant leg.
She may have been the august model for the human female;
there could be no harsh expression before her Olympic face;
the Graces, next to her, would be confounded,
and the sprightly Hours and the sublime Muses
would stop their turns and their song for her.

HYPEAS

She the cause might be of indescribable terror:
for her the Ixionid bows his strong neck.
The human female is the sister of Pain and Death.

CHIRON

By supreme law the hymeneal day will come,
which the dreamer awaits: Caenis will be Caeneus;
the origin of the feminine mystery will be clear:
the Sphinx will tell this secret to her sovereign.

CLITUS

Nature extends her arms and her breasts
to human beings; the key to events
is known to the seer: Homer with his staff,
in her grotto Deiphobe, tongue of the Oracle.

CAUMANTES

The monster expresses a longing from the heart of the Sphere,
the brute in the Centaur absorbs human life,
the satyr is the sacred forest and lust,
he unites sexual impulses to harmonious fury.

Pan junta la soberbia de la montaña agreste
al ritmo de la inmensa mecánica celeste;
la boca melodiosa que atrae en Sirenusa
es de la fiera alada y es de la suave musa;
con la bicorne bestia Pasifae se ayunta,
Naturaleza sabia formas diversas junta,
y cuando tiende al hombre la gran Naturaleza,
el monstruo, siendo el símbolo, se viste de belleza.

GRINEO
Yo amo lo inanimado que amó el divino Hesiodo.

QUIRÓN
Grineo, sobre el mundo tiene un ánima todo.

GRINEO
He visto, entonces, raros ojos fijos en mí:
los vivos ojos rojos del alma del rubí;
los ojos luminosos del alma del topacio
y los de la esmeralda que del azul espacio
la maravilla imitan; los ojos de las gemas
de brillos peregrinos y mágicos emblemas.
Amo el granito duro que el arquitecto labra
y el mármol en que duermen la línea y la palabra . . .

QUIRÓN
A Deucalión y a Pirra, varones y mujeres
las piedras aún intactas dijeron: «¿Qué nos quieres?»

LICIDAS
Yo he visto los lemures flotar, en los nocturnos
instantes, cuando escuchan los bosques taciturnos
el loco grito de Atis que su dolor revela
o la maravillosa canción de Filomela.
El galope apresuro, si en el boscaje miro
manes que pasan, y oigo su fúnebre suspiro.
Pues de la Muerte el hondo, desconocido Imperio,
guarda el pavor sagrado de su fatal misterio.

Pan unites the loftiness of the rustic mountain
to the rhythm of the immense celestial machinery;
the melodious captivating mouth of Sirenusae
is made from the winged beast and the gentle muse;
with the bicorn beast Pasiphaë mated,
wise Nature joins assorted forms together,
and when great Nature makes man lie down,
the monster, being a symbol, puts on beauty.

GRINAEUS

I love the inanimate which the divine Hesiod loved.

CHIRON

Grinaeus, everything on this earth has a soul.

GRINAEUS

I have seen, then, strange eyes staring at me:
the sharp red eyes of the ruby's soul;
the luminous eyes of the topaz's soul
and those of the emerald that imitate
the wonder of blue space; the eyes of gems
of wandering lights and magic emblems.
I love the hard granite which the architect works
and the marble in which the line and the word sleep . . .

CHIRON

To Deucalion and to Pyrrha, men and women,
the stones still intact said, "What do you want from us?"

LYCIDAS

I have seen the Lemures floating, in nocturnal
moments, when the taciturn woods listen
to the mad cry of Attis revealing his pain
or to the marvelous song of Philomela.
I quicken my gallop when I look in the grove
at Manes passing by and hear their dreary sigh.
Death's deep, unknown Empire
retains the holy dread of its fatal mystery.

ARNEO
La Muerte es de la Vida la inseparable hermana.

QUIRÓN
La Muerte es la victoria de la progenie humana.

MEDON
¡La Muerte! Yo la he visto. No es demacrada y mustia
ni ase corva guadaña, ni tiene faz de angustia.
Es semejante a Diana, casta y virgen como ella;
en su rostro hay la gracia de la núbil doncella
y lleva una guirnalda de rosas siderales.
En su siniestra tiene verdes palmas triunfales,
y en su diestra una copa con agua del olvido.
A sus pies, como un perro, yace un amor dormido.

AMICO
Los mismos dioses buscan la dulce paz que vierte.

QUIRÓN
La pena de los dioses es no alcanzar la Muerte.

EURETO
Si el hombre—Prometeo—pudo robar la vida,
la clave de la muerte seréle concedida.

QUIRÓN
La virgen de las vírgenes es inviolable y pura.
Nadie su casto cuerpo tendrá en la alcoba obscura,
ni beberá en sus labios el grito de victoria,
ni arrancará a su frente las rosas de su gloria.
. . . .
* * *

Mas he aquí que Apolo se acerca al meridiano.
Sus truenos prolongados repite el Oceano;
bajo el dorado carro del reluciente Apolo
vuelve a inflar sus carrillos y sus odres Eolo.
A lo lejos, un templo de mármol se divisa

ARNAEUS

Death is Life's inseparable sister.

CHIRON

Death is the victory of human progeny.

MEDON

Death! I have seen her. She is not emaciated and withered,
she neither holds a curved scythe nor has an anguished countenance.
She resembles Diana, chaste and virgin as she;
in her face there is the grace of a nubile maiden
and she wears a garland of sidereal roses.
In her left hand she has green triumphal palms
and in her right, a cup of the waters of oblivion.
At her feet, like a hound, lies a sleeping love.

AMICUS

The very gods seek the sweet peace which she pours out.

CHIRON

The punishment of the gods is not to reach Death.

EURYTUS

If man—Prometheus—was able to steal life,
the key to death will be conceded to him.

CHIRON

The virgin of virgins is inviolable and pure.
None will possess her chaste body in a dark bedroom,
nor drink on her lips the shout of victory,
nor pluck from her brow the roses of her glory.

. . . .

* * *

Yet behold, Apollo approaches the meridian.
The Ocean repeats his prolonged thunderclaps;
beneath the golden cart of gleaming Apollo
Aeolus again puffs out his cheeks and wineskins.
Far away, a marble temple comes into view

entre laureles-rosa que hace cantar la brisa.
Con sus vibrantes notas de Céfiro desgarra
la veste transparente la helénica cigarra,
y por el llano extenso van en tropel sonoro
los Centauros, y al paso, tiembla la Isla de Oro.

LA PÁGINA BLANCA

A A. Lamberti

Mis ojos miraban en hora de ensueños
        la página blanca.

Y vino el desfile de ensueños y sombras.
Y fueron mujeres de rostros de estatua,
mujeres de rostros de estatuas de mármol,
tan tristes, tan dulces, tan suaves, tan pálidas!

Y fueron visiones de extraños poemas,
de extraños poemas de besos y lágrimas,
de historias que dejan en crueles instantes
las testas viriles cubiertas de canas!

Qué cascos de nieve que pone la suerte!
qué arrugas precoces cincela en la cara!
Y cómo se quiere que vayan ligeros
los tardos camellos de la caravana!

Los tardos camellos,—
como las figuras en un panorama,—
cual si fuese un desierto de hielo,
atraviesan la página blanca.

        Este lleva
        una carga
de dolores y angustias antiguas,
angustias de pueblos, dolores de razas;

among rosebays that make the breeze sing.
With its Zephyr-like vibrant notes
the Hellenic cicada rends the transparent cloak,
and over the wide plain in a sonorous throng
go the Centaurs, and as they pass, the Golden Isle trembles.

THE WHITE PAGE

For A. Lamberti

At the daydream hour my eyes were gazing
            at the white page.

And the parade of daydreams and shadows came.
And they were women with statue faces,
women with the faces of marble statues,
so sad, so sweet, so smooth, so pale!

And they were visions of strange poems,
strange poems of kisses and tears,
of stories that left in a cruel instant
virile heads covered in gray!

What snowy helmets fate hands out!
What precocious wrinkles it chisels into the face!
And how one wishes that the listless camels
of the caravan would step lightly!

The listless camels—
like figures in a panorama—,
as if it were a desert of ice,
they cross the white page.

        This one bears
        a load
of age-old pains and woes,
the woes of peoples, the pains of races;

dolores y angustias que sufren los Cristos
que vienen al mundo de víctimas trágicas!

Otro lleva
en la espalda
el cofre de ensueños, de perlas y oro,
que conduce la Reina de Saba.

Otro lleva
una caja
en que va, dolorosa difunta,
como un muerto lirio la pobre Esperanza.

Y camina sobre un dromedario
la Pálida,
la vestida de ropas obscuras,
la Reina invencible, la bella inviolada:
la Muerte.

Y el hombre,
a quien duras visiones asaltan,
el que encuentra en los astros del cielo
prodigios que abruman y signos que espantan,
mira al dromedario
de la caravana
como al mensajero que la luz conduce,
en el vago desierto que forma
la página blanca!

RESPONSO (A VERLAINE)

Padre y maestro mágico, liróforo celeste
que al instrumento olímpico y a la siringa agreste
diste tu acento encantador;
Panida! Pan tú mismo, que coros condujiste
hacia el propíleo sacro que amaba tu alma triste,
al son del sistro y del tambor!

pains and woes suffered by the Christs
who come to this world of tragic victims!

    Another bears
      on its back
the chest of daydreams, of pearls and gold,
which the Queen of Sheba carries.

    Another bears
      a box
in which a sorrowful dead woman travels
like a dead lily: poor Hope.

And traveling on a dromedary comes
      the Pale One,
a woman draped in dark clothing,
the invincible Queen, the inviolate beauty:
      Death.

    And man,
whom cruel visions assault,
who finds in the heavenly bodies
overwhelming prodigies and fearful signs,
      looks at the dromedary
      in the caravan
as if at a messenger carried by the light,
on the vague desert that forms
      the white page!

A PRAYER FOR THE DEAD (TO VERLAINE)

Father and master magician, divine lyre-bearer
who, to the Olympic instrument and the rustic syrinx,
      gave your enchanting accent;
Pandean! You yourself are Pan, who conducted choruses
to the holy Propylaeum, which your sad soul loved,
      to the sound of the sistrum and the drum!

Que tu sepulcro cubra de flores Primavera,
que se humedezca el áspero hocico de la fiera,
        de amor si pasa por allí;
que el fúnebre recinto visite Pan bicorne;
que de sangrientas rosas el fresco Abril te adorne
        y de claveles de rubí.

Que si posarse quiere sobre la tumba el cuervo,
ahuyenten la negrura del pájaro protervo,
        el dulce canto del cristal
que Filomela vierta sobre tus tristes huesos,
o la armonía dulce de risas y de besos,
        de culto oculto y florestal.

Que púberes canéforas te ofrenden el acanto,
que sobre tu sepulcro no se derrame el llanto,
        sino rocío, vino, miel:
que el pámpano allí brote, las flores de Citeres,
y que se escuchen vagos suspiros de mujeres
        bajo un simbólico laurel!

Que si un pastor su pífano bajo el frescor del haya,
en amorosos días, como en Virgilio, ensaya,
        tu nombre ponga en la canción;
y que la virgen náyade, cuando ese nombre escuche,
con ansias y temores entre las linfas luche,
        llena de miedo y de pasión.

De noche, en la montaña, en la negra montaña
de las Visiones, pase gigante sombra extraña,
        sombra de un Sátiro espectral;
que ella al centauro adusto con su grandeza asuste;
de una extra-humana flauta la melodía ajuste
        a la armonía sideral.

Y huya el tropel equino por la montaña vasta;
tu rostro de ultratumba bañe la luna casta
        de compasiva y blanca luz;

May Spring cover your sepulcher with flowers,
may the rugged snout of the wild beast become wet
    with love if it passes there;
may bicorn Pan visit the dreary enclosure;
may fresh April adorn you with bloody roses
    and carnations of ruby.

May these frighten away the black protervity of the crow,
should the bird intend to perch upon your tomb:
    either the sweet song of the crystal
which Philomela will pour upon your sad bones,
or the sweet harmony of laughter and kisses
    from an occult and sylvan cult.

May pubescent canephoroi make you an offering of acanthus,
may your sepulcher not overflow with weeping,
    but with dew, wine, honey:
may the pompano sprout there, the flowers of Cytherea,
and may there be heard the vague sighs of women
    under a symbolic laurel!

May a shepherd—beneath the coolness of the beech,
on love-making days, as in Virgil—playing his fife,
    put your name into his song;
and may the virginal naiad, when she hears this name,
with awe and yearning strive among the lymphs,
    full of fear and passion.

At night, on the mountain, on the black mountain
of Visions, may a strange, gigantic shadow pass,
    the shadow of a spectral Satyr;
may it startle the austere centaur with its grandeur;
may the melody of a flute, beyond human, orchestrate
    the sidereal harmony.

And may the equine throng flee across the vast mountain;
the chaste moon bathe your face from the hereafter
    with white and compassionate light;

y el Sátiro contemple sobre un lejano monte,
una cruz que se eleve cubriendo el horizonte
     y un resplandor sobre la cruz!

PALIMPSESTO

Escrita en viejo dialecto eolio
hallé esta página dentro un infolio
y entre los libros de un monasterio
del venerable San Agustín.
Un fraile acaso puso el escolio
que allí se encuentra; dómine serio
de flacas manos y buen latín.
Hay sus lagunas.

. . . Cuando los toros
de las campañas, bajo los oros
que vierte el hijo de Hiperión,
pasan mugiendo, y en las eternas
rocas salvajes de las cavernas
esperezándose ruge el león;

cuando en las vírgenes y verdes parras
sus secas notas dan las cigarras,
y en los panales de Himeto deja
su rubia carga la leve abeja
que en bocas rojas chupa la miel,
junto a los mirtos, bajo los lauros,
en grupo lírico van los centauros
con la armonía de su tropel.

Uno las patas rítmicas mueve,
otro alza el cuello con gallardía
como en hermoso bajo-relieve
que a golpes mágicos Scopas haría;
otro alza al aire las manos blancas
mientras le dora las finas ancas
con baño cálido la luz del sol;

and the Satyr contemplate, on a distant mountain,
a cross rising to cover the horizon
　　　　and a radiance on the cross!

PALIMPSEST

Written in an old Aeolian dialect
I found this page within a folio
and among the books at a monastery
of the venerable St. Augustine.
A monk perhaps added the gloss
that is found there; an austere schoolmaster
with feeble hands and good Latin.
The lacunae are his.

. . . When the bulls
of the fields, under the gold
which Hyperion's son pours out,
pass lowing, and in the eternal
savage rocks of the caverns
the lion roars as it stretches;

when in the green and virginal grapevines
the cicadas give forth their dry notes,
and in the honeycombs of Hymettus
a blond cargo is dropped off by bees,
which suck the honey in red mouths
beside the myrtles, under the laurels,
in a lyrical band go the centaurs
with the harmony of their throng.

One moves his rhythmic hooves,
another gracefully raises his neck
as if in a lovely bas-relief
which with magical chiseling Scopas would make;
another lifts his white hands into the air
while sunlight bathes his fine haunches
in a hot shower of gold;

y otro saltando piedras y troncos
va dando alegre sus gritos roncos
como el ruido de un caracol.

Silencio. Señas hace ligero
el que en la tropa va delantero;
porque a un recodo de la campaña
llegan en donde Diana se baña.
Se oye el ruido de claras linfas
y la algazara que hacen las ninfas.
Risa de plata que el aire riega
hasta sus ávidos oídos llega;
golpes en la onda, palabras locas,
gritos joviales de frescas bocas,
y los ladridos de la traílla
que Diana tiene junto a la orilla
del fresco río, donde está ella
blanca y desnuda como una estrella.

Tanta blancura que al cisne injuria
abre los ojos de la lujuria:
sobre las márgenes y rocas áridas
vuela el enjambre de las cantáridas
con su bruñido verde metálico,
siempre propicias al culto fálico.
Amplias caderas, pie fino y breve;
las dos colinas de rosa y nieve . . .
cuadro soberbio de tentación!
¡Ay del cuitado que a ver se atreve
lo que fue espanto para Acteón!
Cabellos rubios, mejillas tiernas,
marmóreos cuellos, rosadas piernas,
gracias ocultas del lindo coro,
en el herido cristal sonoro;
seno en que hiciérase sagrada copa;
tal ve en silencio la ardiente tropa.

¿Quién adelanta su firme busto?
¿Quirón experto? ¿Folo robusto?

and another, leaping stones and logs,
is happily launching raucous shouts
like the noise of a seashell.

Silence. The one moving ahead
of the troop makes softer tracks;
because they arrive at a bend
where Diana is bathing.
The noise of clear lymphs is heard
and the frolicking of nymphs.
A silvery laugh, sprinkled
on the breeze, reaches their avid ears;
colliding waves, silly words,
jovial shouts from carefree mouths,
and the yips and barks from the leash
which Diana keeps by the bank
of the cool river, where she is
white and nude as a star.

So much whiteness, which would shame a swan,
opens the eyes of lust:
over the banks and dry rocks
the swarm of cantharides flies,
with their green metallic burnish,
always suitable for the phallic cult.
Ample hips, a fine small foot;
the two hills of rose and snow . . .
a superb picture of temptation!
Alas for the hapless fellow who dares to see
what was a horror for Actaeon!
Blond tresses, tender cheeks,
marmoreal necks, pink legs,
hidden graces of the lovely chorus,
in the wounded, sonorous crystal;
a bosom which might change into a sacred goblet;
this is what in silence the ardent troops see.

Who sticks out his firm torso?
Expert Chiron? Robust Pholus?

Es el más joven y es el más bello;
su piel es blanca, crespo el cabello,
los cascos finos, y en la mirada
brilla del sátiro la llamarada.
En un instante, veloz y listo,
a una tan bella como Kalisto,
ninfa que a la alta diosa acompaña,
saca de la onda donde se baña:
la grupa vuelve, raudo galopa;
tal iba el toro raptor de Europa
con el orgullo de su conquista.

¿A do va Diana? Viva la vista,
la planta alada, la cabellera
mojada y suelta; terrible, fiera,
corre del monte por la extensión;
ladran sus perros enfurecidos;
entre sus dedos humedecidos
lleva una flecha para el ladrón.

Ya a los centauros a ver alcanza
la cazadora; ya el dardo lanza,
y un grito se oye de hondo dolor:
la casta diva de la venganza
mató al raptor . . .
La tropa rápida se esparce huyendo,
forman los cascos sonoro estruendo.
Llegan las ninfas. Lloran. ¿Qué ven?
En la carrera la cazadora
con su saeta castigadora
a la robada mató también.

COSAS DEL CID

A Francisco A. de Icaza

Cuenta Barbey, en versos que valen bien su prosa
una hazaña del Cid, fresca como una rosa,

He is the youngest and he the most beautiful;
his skin is white, matted his hair,
the hooves fine, and in his gaze
the blaze of the satyr shimmers.
In an instant, quick and clever,
he snatches from the wave where she bathes
one as beautiful as Callisto,
a nymph who escorts the lofty goddess:
the crupper turns, swiftly he gallops;
so would run the bull that abducted Europa,
with the pride of his conquest.

Whither goes Diana? Her eyes sharp,
her foot winged, her tresses
damp and loose; terrible, wild,
she covers the expanse of the mountain;
her furious dogs are barking;
between her wet fingers
she holds an arrow for the thief.

Now the huntress catches sight
of the centaurs; now the dart flies,
and a cry of deep pain is heard:
the chaste goddess of vengeance
slew the abductor . . .
The swift band scatters in flight,
the hooves make a thunderous commotion.
The nymphs arrive. They weep. What do they see?
In the mad dash the huntress
with her punishing shaft
has slain the abducted nymph as well.

CONCERNING THE CID

For Francisco A. de Icaza

Barbey tells, in verses worthy of his prose,
a feat of the Cid, fresh as a rose,

pura como una perla. No se oyen en la hazaña
resonar en el viento las trompetas de España,
ni el azorado moro las tiendas abandona
al ver al sol el alma de acero de Tizona.

Babieca descansando del huracán guerrero,
tranquilo pace, mientras el bravo caballero
sale a gozar del aire de la estación florida.
Ríe la Primavera, y el vuelo de la vida
abre lirios y sueños en el jardín del mundo.
Rodrigo de Vivar pasa, meditabundo,
por una senda en donde, bajo el sol glorioso,
tendiéndole la mano, le detiene un leproso.

Frente a frente, el soberbio príncipe del estrago
y la victoria, joven, bello como Santiago,
y el horror animado, la viviente carroña
que infecta los suburbios de hedor y de ponzoña.

Y al Cid tiende la mano el siniestro mendigo,
y su escarcela busca y no encuentra Rodrigo.
—¡Oh Cid, una limosna!— dice el precito.

                                —Hermano
te ofrezco la desnuda limosna de mi mano!—
dice el Cid; y, quitando su férreo guante, extiende
la diestra al miserable, que llora y que comprende.

         *   *   *

Tal es el sucedido que el Condestable escancia
como un vino precioso en su copa de Francia.
Yo agregaré este sorbo de licor castellano:

         *   *   *

Cuando su guantelete hubo vuelto a la mano
el Cid, siguió su rumbo por la primaveral
senda. Un pájaro daba su nota de cristal
en un árbol. El cielo profundo deslëía
un perfume de gracia en la gloria del día.
Las ermitas lanzaban en el aire sonoro
su melodiosa lluvia de tórtolas de oro;
el alma de las flores iba por los caminos

pure as a pearl. In this feat the trumpets of Spain
are not heard resounding in the wind,
nor does the frightened Moor abandon his tents
upon seeing in the sun Tizona's steel soul.

Babieca, resting from the hurricane of war,
grazes peacefully while the valiant knight
steps out to enjoy the air in the flowery season.
Springtime laughs, and the flight of life
opens lilies and dreams in the garden of the world.
Rodrigo de Vivar pensively walks
along a path where, beneath the glorious sun,
a leper stops him by holding out a hand.

Face to face, the superb prince of havoc
and victory, young, beautiful as St. James,
and the animated horror, the living carrion
that infects the outskirts of town with stench and poison.

And to the Cid this sinister beggar extends his hand,
and Rodrigo looks for his purse in vain.
"O Cid, an alms!" says the poor devil.
                              "Brother,
I offer you the naked alms of my hand!"
says the Cid; and, removing his ferrous glove, puts out
his right hand to the wretch, who weeps and who understands.
                    *   *   *
Such is the event which the High Constable pours
like a costly wine in his glass of France.
I will add this sip of Castilian liqueur:
                    *   *   *
When the gauntlet had returned to his hand,
the Cid went his way on the springtime
path. A bird let out a crystal note
in a tree. The deep sky dissolved
a charming perfume in the glory of the day.
The hermitages cast into the sonorous air
their melodious rain of golden turtledoves;
the soul of the flowers took to the roads

a unirse a la piadosa voz de los peregrinos,
y el gran Rodrigo Díaz de Vivar, satisfecho,
iba cual si llevase una estrella en el pecho.
Cuando de la campiña, aromada de esencia
sutil, salió una niña vestida de inocencia,
una niña que fuera una mujer, de franca
y angélica pupila, y muy dulce y muy blanca.
Una niña que fuera un hada, o que surgiera
encarnación de la divina Primavera.

Y fue al Cid y le dijo: «Alma de amor y fuego,
por Jimena y por Dios un regalo te entrego,
esta rosa naciente y este fresco laurel.»

Y el Cid, sobre su yelmo las frescas hojas siente,
en su guante de hierro hay una flor naciente,
y en lo íntimo del alma como un dulzor de miel.

AMA TU RITMO . . .

Ama tu ritmo y ritma tus acciones
bajo su ley, así como tus versos;
eres un universo de universos
y tu alma una fuente de canciones.

La celeste unidad que presupones
hará brotar en ti mundos diversos,
y al resonar tus números dispersos
pitagoriza en tus constelaciones.

Escucha la retórica divina
del pájaro del aire y la nocturna
irradiación geométrica adivina;

mata la indiferencia taciturna
y engarza perla y perla cristalina
en donde la verdad vuelca su urna.

to join the pious voices of the pilgrims,
and the great Rodrigo Díaz de Vivar, satisfied,
walked along as if carrying a star on his chest.
When from the countryside, perfumed with a subtle
essence, a girl came dressed in innocence,
a girl who might have been a woman, of forthright
and angelic eyes, and very sweet and very white.
A girl who might have been a fairy, or might suggest
the incarnation of divine Springtime.

And she went up to the Cid and said: "Soul of love and fire,
for Ximena's sake and God's I present you
with this budding rose and this fresh-cut laurel."

And the Cid feels on his helmet the fresh leaves,
in his iron glove there is a budding flower,
and in his innermost soul a sweetness of honey.

LOVE YOUR RHYTHM . . .

Love your rhythm and give rhythm to your actions
under its law, as well as to your verses;
you are a universe of universes
and your soul a fountain of songs.

The celestial unity which you work out
will make many worlds burgeon in you,
and when your scattered numbers resound,
pythagorize upon your constellations.

Heed the divine rhetoric
of the bird of the air, and divine
the nocturnal geometric irradiation;

kill taciturn indifference
and link pearl to crystalline pearl
where the truth tips over its urn.

YO PERSIGO UNA FORMA . . .

Yo persigo una forma que no encuentra mi estilo,
botón de pensamiento que busca ser la rosa;
se anuncia con un beso que en mis labios se posa
al abrazo imposible de la Venus de Milo.

Adornan verdes palmas el blanco peristilo;
los astros me han predicho la visión de la Diosa;
y en mi alma reposa la luz como reposa
el ave de la luna sobre un lago tranquilo.

Y no hallo sino la palabra que huye,
la iniciación melódica que de la flauta fluye
y la barca del sueño que en el espacio boga;

y bajo la ventana de mi Bella-Durmiente,
el sollozo continuo del chorro de la fuente
y el cuello del gran cisne blanco que me interroga.

I PURSUE A FORM . . .

I pursue a form that my style does not find,
a bud of thought that seeks to be a rose;
it announces itself with a kiss that alights on my lips
in the impossible embrace of the Venus de Milo.

Green palms adorn the white peristyle;
the stars have predicted for me the vision of the Goddess;
and the light reposes in my soul as the bird
of the moon reposes on a tranquil lake.

And I find nothing but the word that gets away,
the melodic initiation that flows from the flute,
and the ship of sleep that sails into space;

and under the window of my Sleeping Beauty,
the continuous sob of the fountain's jet
and the great white swan's neck questioning me.

CERTÁMEN VARELA

OBRAS PREMIADAS

I DISTINGUIDAS

Entre las novecientas noventa composiciones presentadas al certámen literario
promovido en 1887

POR EL

Señor Don Federico Varela

Senador por la provincia de Valparaiso

..o◊o..

EDICION HECHA A SUS ESPENSAS

TOMO PRIMERO

ANTOLOJÍA

[signature: Belisario Guzman Campos]

SANTIAGO DE CHILE

IMPRENTA CERVANTES

CALLE DE LA BANDERA, NÚM. 73

—

1887

Front cover of the volume that included Darío's *Rimas,* along with several other poems presented for a literary contest in 1887 in Chile.

Cantos de vida y esperanza. Los cisnes y otros poemas.
(1905)

A Nicaragua. A la República Argentina.
R.D.

Prefacio

Podría repetir aquí más de un concepto de las palabras liminares de *Prosas profanas*. Mi respeto por la aristocracia del pensamiento, por la nobleza del Arte, siempre es el mismo. Mi antiguo aborrecimiento a la mediocridad, a la mulatez intelectual, a la chatura estética, apenas si se aminora hoy con una razonada indiferencia.

El movimiento de libertad que me tocó iniciar en América, se propagó hasta España y tanto aquí como allá el triunfo está logrado. Aunque respecto a técnica tuviese demasiado que decir en el país en donde la expresión poética está anquilosada a punto de que la momificación del ritmo ha llegado a ser un artículo de fe, no haré sino una corta advertencia. En todos los países cultos de Europa se ha usado del hexámetro absolutamente clásico sin que la mayoría letrada y sobre todo la minoría leída se asustasen de semejante manera de cantar. En Italia ha mucho tiempo, sin citar antiguos, que Carducci ha autorizado los hexámetros; en inglés, no me atrevería casi a indicar, por respeto a la cultura de mis lectores, que la *Evangelina* de Longfellow está en los mismos versos en que Horacio dijo sus mejores pensares. En cuanto al verso libre moderno . . . ¿no es verdaderamente singular que en esta tierra de Quevedos y de Góngoras los únicos innovadores del instrumento lírico, los únicos libertadores del ritmo, hayan sido los poetas del *Madrid Cómico* y los libretistas del género chico?

Hago esta advertencia porque la forma es lo que primeramente toca a las muchedumbres. Yo no soy un poeta para muchedumbres. Pero sé que indefectiblemente tengo que ir a ellas.

Cuando dije que mi poesía era «mía, en mí» sostuve la primera condición de mi existir, sin pretensión ninguna de causar sectarismo en mente o voluntad ajena, y en un intenso amor a lo absoluto de la belleza.

Al seguir la vida que Dios me ha concedido tener, he buscado expresarme lo más noble y altamente en mi comprensión; voy diciendo mi verso con una modestia tan orgullosa que solamente las espigas comprenden, y cultivo, entre otras flores, una rosa rosada, concreción de alba, capullo de porvenir, entre el bullicio de la literatura.

SONGS OF LIFE AND HOPE. THE SWANS AND OTHER POEMS
(1905)

For Nicaragua. For the Argentine Republic.
R.D.

PREFACE

I could repeat here more than one concept from the liminary words of *Prosas profanas.* My respect for the aristocracy of thought, for the nobility of Art, remains the same. My former abhorrence of mediocrity, of intellectual mongrelizing, of esthetic shallowness, has scarcely subsided today with reasoned indifference.

The freedom movement which I happened to initiate in America has spread to Spain, and as much here as there, its triumph is assured. Although I have far more to say in a country in which poetic expression is ankylosed to the point where mummification of rhythm has become an article of faith, I will give but one small word of warning regarding technique. In all cultured countries of Europe they have used the utterly classical hexameter without scaring off the educated majority and, most of all, the reading minority from a similar way of singing. For a while now, Carducci (not to mention earlier poets) has made the hexameter acceptable in Italy; out of respect for the culture of my readers, I hardly dare to point out that, in English, Longfellow's *Evangeline* is composed of the same verses in which Horace spoke his best thoughts. As for modern free verse . . . Is it not truly odd that in this land of Quevedos and Góngoras the only innovators of the lyrical instrument, the only liberators of rhythm, have been the poets of the *Madrid Cómico* and the librettists of the popular stage?

I give this word of warning because form is what primarily touches the masses. I am not a poet for the masses. But I know that inevitably I must go to them.

When I said that my poetry was "mine, in me," I upheld the first condition of my existence, with no pretense at all of causing sectarianism in the mind or intention of others, but with an intense love for the absolute nature of beauty.

In pursuing the life which God has granted me to live, I have sought to express myself to the highest and most noble extent I know how; I start speaking my verse with a modesty so full of pride that only the ears of wheat can understand, and I cultivate, among other flowers, a rosy rose, the concretion of a dawn, the bud of what is to come, amid the bedlam of literature.

Si en estos cantos hay política, es porque aparece universal. Y si encontráis versos a un presidente, es porque son un clamor continental. Mañana podremos ser yanquis (y es lo más probable); de todas maneras mi protesta queda, escrita sobre las alas de los inmaculados cisnes, tan ilustres como Júpiter.

R.D.

Yo soy aquel . . .

Yo soy aquel que ayer no más decía
el verso azul y la canción profana,
en cuya noche un ruiseñor había
que era alondra de luz por la mañana.

El dueño fui de mi jardín de sueño,
lleno de rosas y de cisnes vagos;
el dueño de las tórtolas, el dueño
de góndolas y liras en los lagos;

y muy siglo diez y ocho y muy antiguo
y muy moderno; audaz, cosmopolita;
con Hugo fuerte y con Verlaine ambiguo,
y una sed de ilusiones infinita.

Yo supe de dolor desde mi infancia,
mi juventud . . . ¿fue juventud la mía?
sus rosas aún me dejan su fragancia,—
una fragancia de melancolía . . .

Potro sin freno se lanzó mi instinto,
mi juventud montó potro sin freno;
iba embriagada y con puñal al cinto;
si no cayó, fue porque Dios es bueno.

En mi jardín se vio una estatua bella;
se juzgó mármol y era carne viva;
un alma joven habitaba en ella,
sentimental, sensible, sensitiva.

If in these songs there is politics, it is because politics appears universally. And if you find verses to a president, it is because they are a continental clamor. Tomorrow we may well become Yankees (and this is most likely); my protest stands anyhow, written on the wings of immaculate swans, as illustrious as Jupiter.

R.D.

I AM THE ONE . . .

I am the one who just yesterday spoke
the blue verse and the profane song,
in whose night there was a nightingale
that was a skylark of light in the morning.

I was the master of my dream garden
full of roses and vague swans;
the master of turtledoves, the master
of gondolas and lyres on the lakes;

and very eighteenth-century and very old-fashioned
and very modern; audacious, cosmopolitan;
with stalwart Hugo and ambiguous Verlaine,
and an infinite thirst for dreams.

I've learned of pain since my childhood,
my youth . . . Was mine a youth?
Its roses still leave me its fragrance,
a fragrance of melancholy . . .

An unbridled colt, my instinct rushed on,
my youth rode an unbridled colt;
it passed intoxicated and with a dagger in its belt;
if it didn't fall, it was because God is good.

In my garden was a beautiful statue;
it was thought to be marble, and was living flesh;
a young soul lived within it,
sentimental, sensitive, susceptible.

Y tímida ante el mundo, de manera
que encerrada en silencio no salía,
sino cuando en la dulce primavera
era la hora de la melodía . . .

Hora de ocaso y de discreto beso;
hora crepuscular y de retiro;
hora de madrigal y de embeleso,
de «te adoro», de «ay» y de suspiro.

Y entonces era en la dulzaina un juego
de misteriosas gamas cristalinas,
un renovar de notas del Pan griego
y un desgranar de músicas latinas,

con aire tal y con ardor tan vivo,
que a la estatua nacían de repente
en el muslo viril patas de chivo
y dos cuernos de sátiro en la frente.

Como la Galatea gongorina
me encantó la marquesa verleniana,
y así juntaba a la pasión divina
una sensual hiperestesia humana;

todo ansia, todo ardor, sensación pura
y vigor natural; y sin falsía,
y sin comedia y sin literatura . . . :
si hay un alma sincera, ésa es la mía.

La torre de marfil tentó mi anhelo;
quise encerrarme dentro de mí mismo,
y tuve hambre de espacio y sed de cielo
desde las sombras de mi propio abismo.

Como la esponja que la sal satura
en el jugo del mar, fue el dulce y tierno
corazón mío, henchido de amargura
por el mundo, la carne y el infierno.

And shy before the world, so
that, locked in silence, it wouldn't come out,
except in the sweet spring
when it was time for melody . . .

Time for sunset and a discreet kiss;
time for twilight and seclusion;
time for madrigal and enchantment,
for "I adore you," for "oh no," and for a sigh.

And then on the pipes it was a game
of mysterious crystalline scales,
a renewing of notes from the Greek Pan,
and a threshing of Latin music,

with such an air and a fervor so alive
that on the statue suddenly goat feet
would sprout from the virile thigh
and two satyr horns from the brow.

As much as the Galatea of Góngora
I loved the Marquise of Verlaine,
and so combined divine passion
with a sensuous human hyperesthesia;

every longing, every fervor, a pure sensation
and natural vigor; with no insincerity,
and no comedy and no literature . . . :
if there is an honest soul, it is mine.

The ivory tower tempted my desires;
I tried to lock myself within me,
and got hungry for space and thirsty for sky
from the shadows of my own abyss.

Like a sponge saturated by salt
in the juice of the sea, was this sweet and tender
heart of mine, swollen with bitterness
by the world, the flesh, and hell.

Mas, por gracia de Dios, en mi conciencia
el Bien supo elegir la mejor parte;
y si hubo áspera hiel en mi existencia,
melificó toda acritud el Arte.

Mi intelecto libré de pensar bajo,
bañó el agua castalia el alma mía,
peregrinó mi corazón y trajo
de la sagrada selva la armonía.

¡Oh, la selva sagrada! ¡Oh, la profunda
emanación del corazón divino
de la sagrada selva! ¡Oh, la fecunda
fuente cuya virtud vence al destino!

Bosque ideal que lo real complica,
allí el cuerpo arde y vive y Psiquis vuela;
mientras abajo el sátiro fornica,
ebria de azul deslíe Filomela

perla de ensueño y música amorosa
en la cúpula en flor del laurel verde,
Hipsipila sutil liba en la rosa,
y la boca del fauno el pezón muerde.

Allí va el dios en celo tras la hembra,
y la caña de Pan se alza del lodo;
la eterna Vida sus semillas siembra,
y brota la armonía del gran Todo.

El alma que entra allí debe ir desnuda,
temblando de deseo y fiebre santa,
sobre cardo heridor y espina aguda:
así sueña, así vibra y así canta.

Vida, luz y verdad, tal triple llama
produce la interior llama infinita;
el Arte puro como Cristo exclama:
Ego sum lux et veritas et vita!

Yet, by the grace of God, in my consciousness
Good learned to choose the better part;
and if there was bitter gall in my existence,
Art made honey of every acridity.

I freed my intellect from base thinking,
the waters of Castalia bathed my soul,
my heart made a pilgrimage and brought
harmony from the sacred wood.

Oh, the sacred wood! Oh, the profound
emanation of the divine heart
of the sacred wood! Oh, the fecund
fountain whose virtue overcomes fate!

Ideal forest that complicates the real,
there the body burns and lives and Psyche flies;
while the satyr fornicates below,
Philomela—drunk on blue—dissolves

pearls of fantasy and amorous music
in the cupola of the flowering green laurel,
subtle Hypsipyle sucks on the rose,
and the mouth of the faun bites her nipple.

There the god goes in heat after the female,
and Pan's reed rises from the mud;
eternal Life sows its seeds,
and harmony springs from the great All.

The soul that enters there should go naked,
trembling with desire and holy fever,
over wounding thistle and pointed thorn:
so it dreams, so it vibrates, and so it sings.

Life, light, and truth, like a triple flame
produces the infinite inner flame;
pure Art like Christ exclaims:
Ego sum lux et veritas et vita!

Y la vida es misterio; la luz ciega
y la verdad inaccesible asombra;
la adusta perfección jamás se entrega,
y el secreto Ideal duerme en la sombra.

Por eso ser sincero es ser potente.
De desnuda que está, brilla la estrella;
el agua dice el alma de la fuente
en la voz de cristal que fluye d'ella.

Tal fue mi intento, hacer del alma pura
mía, una estrella, una fuente sonora,
con el horror de la literatura
y loco de crepúsculo y de aurora.

Del crepúsculo azul que da la pauta
que los celestes éxtasis inspira,
bruma y tono menor—¡toda la flauta!,
y Aurora, hija del Sol—¡toda la lira!

Pasó una piedra que lanzó una honda;
pasó una flecha que aguzó un violento.
La piedra de la honda fue a la onda,
y la flecha del odio fuese al viento.

La virtud está en ser tranquilo y fuerte;
con el fuego interior todo se abrasa;
se triunfa del rencor y de la muerte,
y hacia Belén . . . la caravana pasa!

A ROOSEVELT

Es con voz de la Biblia, o verso de Walt Whitman,
que habría que llegar hasta ti, Cazador!
Primitivo y moderno, sencillo y complicado,
con un algo de Washington y cuatro de Nemrod!
Eres los Estados Unidos,
eres el futuro invasor

And life is a mystery; light blinds
and inaccessible truth bewilders;
austere perfection never yields,
and the secret Ideal sleeps in the shadow.

Thus, to be sincere is to be powerful.
As naked as it is, the star shines;
water expresses the fountain's soul
in the crystal voice that flows from it.

Such was my intent, to turn this pure soul
of mine into a star, a sonorous fountain,
with the horror of literature
and mad about dusk and dawn.

About the blue dusk that sets the standard,
inspiring heavenly ecstasies;
fog and a minor key: the whole flute!
And Aurora, daughter of the sun: the whole lyre!

A stone went flying from a slingshot;
an arrow, which a violent man had sharpened, flew.
The stone from the slingshot went into the wave,
and the arrow of hate went off to the wind.

Virtue lies in being tranquil and strong;
with inner fire everything burns;
one triumphs over spite and over death,
and on to Bethlehem . . . the caravan passes!

To Roosevelt

It would take a voice from the Bible or a verse from Walt Whitman
to get through to you, Hunter!
Primitive and modern, simple and complicated,
one part Washington and four parts Nimrod!
You're the United States,
you're the future invader

de la América ingenua que tiene sangre indígena,
que aún reza a Jesucristo y aún habla en español.

Eres soberbio y fuerte ejemplar de tu raza;
eres culto, eres hábil; te opones a Tolstoy.
Y domando caballos, o asesinando tigres,
eres un Alejandro-Nabucodonosor.
(Eres un Profesor de Energía
como dicen los locos de hoy).

Crees que la vida es incendio,
que el progreso es erupción;
que en donde pones la bala
el porvenir pones.

                         No.

Los Estados Unidos son potentes y grandes.
Cuando ellos se estremecen hay un hondo temblor
que pasa por las vértebras enormes de los Andes.
Si clamáis se oye como el rugir del león.
Ya Hugo a Grant lo dijo: Las estrellas son vuestras.
(Apenas brilla, alzándose, el argentino sol
y la estrella chilena se levanta . . .) Sois ricos.
Juntáis al culto de Hércules el culto de Mammón;
y alumbrando el camino de la fácil conquista,
la Libertad levanta su antorcha en Nueva-York.

Mas la América nuestra, que tenía poetas
desde los viejos tiempos de Netzahualcoyotl,
que ha guardado las huellas de los pies del gran Baco,
que el alfabeto pánico en un tiempo aprendió;
que consultó los astros, que conoció la Atlántida
cuyo nombre nos llega resonando en Platón,
que desde los remotos momentos de su vida
vive de luz, de fuego, de perfume, de amor,
la América del grande Moctezuma, del Inca,
la América fragante de Cristóbal Colón,
la América católica, la América española,

of the guileless America of indigenous blood
that still prays to Jesus Christ and still speaks in Spanish.

You're a strong and splendid specimen of your kind;
you're cultured, you're skillful; you're the opposite of Tolstoy.
And breaking horses or slaying tigers,
you're an Alexander-Nebuchadnezzar.
(You're a Professor of Energy,
as the madmen of today put it.)

You think that life is a conflagration,
that progress is an eruption,
that where you put your bullet
you set the future.

No.

The United States is powerful and big.
When it shudders, a deep earthquake
runs down the enormous vertebrae of the Andes.
If you cry out, it's heard like the roaring of a lion.
Once Hugo said to Grant: "The stars are yours."
(The Argentine sun, now dawning, has hardly begun to shine,
and the Chilean star is rising . . .) You're rich.
You combine the worship of Hercules with the worship of Mammon;
and lighting the way for easy conquest,
Liberty raises her torch in New York.

Yet this America of ours, which has had poets
since the olden days of Netzahualcoyotl,
which preserves the footprints of great Bacchus,
which once learned the Panic alphabet;
which consulted the stars, which knew the Atlantis
whose name comes down to us loud and clear in Plato,
which from the first moments of life, so long ago,
has lived on light, on fire, on perfume, on love,
the America of the great Montezuma, of the Inca,
the fragrant America of Christopher Columbus,
Catholic America, Spanish America,

la América en que dijo el noble Guatemoc:
«Yo no estoy en un lecho de rosas»; esa América
que tiembla de huracanes y que vive de amor;
hombres de ojos sajones y alma bárbara, vive.
Y sueña. Y ama, y vibra; y es la hija del Sol.
Tened cuidado. Vive la América española!
Hay mil cachorros sueltos del León Español.
Se necesitaría, Roosevelt, ser por Dios mismo,
el Riflero terrible y el fuerte Cazador,
para poder tenernos en vuestras férreas garras.

Y, pues contáis con todo, falta una cosa: Dios!

TORRES DE DIOS! . . .

Torres de Dios! Poetas!
Pararrayos celestes,
que resistís las duras tempestades,
como crestas escuetas,
como picos agrestes,
rompeolas de las eternidades!

La mágica Esperanza anuncia un día
en que sobre la roca de armonía
expirará la pérfida sirena.
Esperad, esperemos todavía!

Esperad todavía.
El bestial elemento se solaza
en el odio a la sacra poesía
y se arroja baldón de raza a raza.
La insurrección de abajo
tiende a los Excelentes.
El caníbal codicia su tasajo
con roja encía y afilados dientes.

Torres, poned al pabellón sonrisa.
Poned ante ese mal y ese recelo,

the America where the noble Cuauhtemoc said:
"This is no bed of roses"; that America
which shakes with hurricanes and lives on love;
men with Saxon eyes and barbarous souls, it lives.
And dreams. And loves, and quivers, and is the daughter of the Sun.
Beware. Spanish America lives!
There are a thousand cubs set loose from the Spanish Lion.
For God's sake, one would need to be, Roosevelt,
a terrifying Sharpshooter and a mighty Hunter
to hold us in your ferrous claws.

And, even accounting for everything, you lack one thing: God!

TOWERS OF GOD! . . .

Towers of God! Poets!
Heavenly lightning rods
that resist severe tempests,
like unadorned crests,
like rustic peaks,
breakwaters of eternities!

Magical Hope announces the day
when on the rock of harmony
the perfidious siren will expire.
You must have hope, let's still hope!

You must still have hope.
The bestial element takes comfort
in the hatred for sacred poetry,
hurling insults of all kinds.
The revolt from below
spreads to the highborn.
The cannibal covets his piece of meat
with red gums and sharpened teeth.

Towers, put a smile on the flag.
In the face of that evil and that misgiving

una soberbia insinuación de brisa
y una tranquilidad de mar y cielo . . .

SPES

Jesús, incomparable perdonador de injurias,
óyeme; Sembrador de trigo, dame el tierno
Pan de tus hostias; dame, contra el sañudo infierno
una gracia lustral de iras y lujurias.

Dime que este espantoso horror de la agonía
que me obsede, es no más de mi culpa nefanda,
que al morir hallaré la luz de un nuevo día
y que entonces oiré mi «Levántate y anda!»

QUÉ SIGNO HACES . . . ?

Qué signo haces, oh Cisne, con tu encorvado cuello
al paso de los tristes y errantes soñadores?
Por qué tan silencioso de ser blanco y ser bello,
tiránico a las aguas e impasible a las flores?

Yo te saludo ahora como en versos latinos
te saludara antaño Publio Ovidio Nasón.
Los mismos ruiseñores cantan los mismos trinos,
y en diferentes lenguas es la misma canción.

A vosotros mi lengua no debe ser extraña.
A Garcilaso visteis, acaso, alguna vez . . .
Soy un hijo de América, soy un nieto de España . . .
Quevedo pudo hablaros en verso en Aranjuez . . .

Cisnes, los abanicos de vuestras alas frescas
den a las frentes pálidas sus caricias más puras
y alejen vuestras blancas figuras pintorescas
de nuestras mentes tristes las ideas obscuras.

put the lofty suggestion of a breeze
and the tranquillity of sea and sky . . .

SPES

Jesus, incomparable forgiver of trespasses,
hear me; Sower of wheat, give me the tender
Bread of your hosts; give me, in the face of furious hell,
a lustral grace from rages and lusts.

Tell me that this appalling horror of agony
that obsesses me, comes only from my heinous guilt,
that on dying I will find the light of a new day
and will then hear my "Rise up and walk!"

WHAT SIGN DO YOU GIVE . . . ?

What sign do you give, O Swan, with your curving neck
when the sad and wandering dreamers pass?
Why so silent from being white and being beautiful,
tyrannical to the waters and impassive to the flowers?

I greet you now as in Latin verses
Publius Ovid Naso greeted you in years gone by.
The same nightingales sing the same trills,
and in different languages it is the same song.

To you my language should not be foreign.
Perhaps you saw Garcilaso at some point . . .
I am a son of America, I am a grandson of Spain . . .
Quevedo was able to speak to you in verse in Aranjuez . . .

Swans, may the fans of your cool wings
give to pallid brows their purest caresses
and may your white picturesque figures
drive the dark ideas from our sad minds.

Brumas septentrionales nos llenan de tristezas,
se mueren nuestras rosas, se agotan nuestras palmas,
casi no hay ilusiones para nuestras cabezas,
y somos los mendigos de nuestras pobres almas.

Nos predican la guerra con águilas feroces,
gerifaltes de antaño revienen a los puños,
mas no brillan las glorias de las antiguas hoces,
ni hay Rodrigos, ni Jaimes, ni hay Alfonsos ni Nuños.

Faltos de los alientos que dan las grandes cosas,
qué haremos los poetas sino buscar tus lagos?
A falta de laureles son muy dulces las rosas,
y a falta de victorias busquemos los halagos.

La América española como la España entera
fija está en el Oriente de su fatal destino;
yo interrogo a la Esfinge que el porvenir espera
con la interrogación de tu cuello divino.

¿Seremos entregados a los bárbaros fieros?
Tantos millones de hombres hablaremos inglés?
Ya no hay nobles hidalgos ni bravos caballeros?
Callaremos ahora para llorar después?

He lanzado mi grito, Cisnes, entre vosotros
que habéis sido los fieles en la desilusión,
mientras siento una fuga de americanos potros
y el estertor postrero de un caduco león . . .

. . . Y un cisne negro dijo: —«La noche anuncia el día».
Y uno blanco: —«La aurora es inmortal! la aurora
es inmortal!» Oh tierras de sol y de armonía,
aún guarda la Esperanza la caja de Pandora!

Septentrional mists fill us with sorrows,
our roses are killed off, our palm trees used up,
there is scarecely a dream for our heads,
and we are beggars of our poor souls.

They preach war to us with ferocious eagles,
gyrfalcons of bygone days return to the fists,
yet the glories of the old sickles do not shine,
there are no Rodrigos nor Jaimes, no Alfonsos nor Nuños.

At a loss for the vital spirit which great things give,
what will we poets do, but seek out your lakes?
For lack of laurels, roses are very sweet,
and for lack of victories, let's seek out adulation.

Spanish America, like Spain as a whole,
is set in the East of its fatal destiny;
I question the Sphinx that awaits the future
with the question mark of your divine neck.

Will we be handed over to the wild barbarians?
So many millions of men, will we be speaking English?
Are there no worthy nobles nor manly knights anymore?
Will we be silent now only to weep later?

I have raised my cry, Swans, among you
who were the faithful in the face of disappointment,
while I hear a stampede of American colts
and the final agony of a senile lion . . .

. . . And a black swan said: "Night foretells the day."
And a white one: "The dawn is immortal! The dawn
is immortal!" O lands of sun and of harmony,
Pandora's box still holds Hope!

POR UN MOMENTO . . .

Por un momento, oh Cisne, juntaré mis anhelos
a los de tus dos alas que abrazaron a Leda,
y a mi maduro ensueño, aún vestido de seda,
dirás, por los Dioscuros, la gloria de los cielos.

Es el otoño. Ruedan de la flauta consuelos.
Por un instante, oh Cisne, en la obscura alameda
sorberé entre dos labios lo que el Pudor me veda,
y dejaré mordidos Escrúpulos y Celos.

Cisne, tendré tus alas blancas por un instante,
y el corazón de rosa que hay en tu dulce pecho
palpitará en el mío con su sangre constante.

Amor será dichoso, pues estará vibrante
el júbilo que pone al gran Pan en acecho
mientras su ritmo esconde la fuente de diamante.

POR EL INFLUJO DE LA PRIMAVERA

Sobre el jarrón de cristal
hay flores nuevas. Anoche
hubo una lluvia de besos.
Despertó un fauno bicorne
tras un alma sensitiva.
Dieron su olor muchas flores.
En la pasional siringa
brotaron las siete voces
que en siete carrizos puso
Pan.

Antiguos ritos paganos
se renovaron. La estrella
de Venus brilló más límpida
y diamantina. Las fresas
del bosque dieron su sangre.

FOR JUST A MOMENT . . .

For just a moment, O Swan, I will link my longings
to those of your two wings, which embraced Leda;
and to my middle-aged fantasy, still dressed in silk,
you will tell, for the Dioscouri, the glory of the skies.

It is autumn. Consolation tumbles from the flute.
For just an instant, O Swan, in the dark poplar grove
I will sip between two lips what Modesty forbids me,
and will leave Scruples and Jealousy bitten off.

Swan, I will have your white wings for just an instant,
and the rose heart that is there in your sweet breast
will throb in mine with its steady blood.

Love will be blissful, since the jubilation,
which gets the great Pan peeking, will be vibrant
while its rhythm conceals the diamond fountain.

BECAUSE OF THE INFLUENCE OF SPRING

Above the crystal vase
there are new flowers. Last night
there was a shower of kisses.
It awoke a bicorn faun
in pursuit of a sensitive soul.
Many flowers gave their scent.
From the passional syrinx
sprouted the seven voices
that were placed in seven reeds
by Pan.

Ancient pagan rites
were renewed. The star
of Venus shone more limpid
and adamantine. The strawberries
of the wood gave their blood.

El nido estuvo de fiesta.
Un ensueño florentino
se enfloró de primavera,
de modo que en carne viva
renacieron ansias muertas.
Imaginaos un roble
que diera una rosa fresca;
un buen egipán latino
con una bacante griega
y parisiense. Una música
magnífica. Una suprema
inspiración primitiva,
llena de cosas modernas.
Un vasto orgullo viril
que aroma el *odor di femina*;
un trono de roca en donde
descansa un lirio.

Divina Estación! Divina
Estación! Sonríe el alba
más dulcemente. La cola
del pavo real exalta
su prestigio. El sol aumenta
su íntima influencia; y el arpa
de los nervios vibra sola.
Oh, Primavera sagrada!
Oh, gozo del don sagrado
de la vida! Oh, bella palma
sobre nuestras frentes! Cuello
del cisne! Paloma blanca!
Rosa roja! Palio azul!
Y todo por ti, oh, alma!
Y por ti, cuerpo, y por ti,
idea, que los enlazas.
Y por Ti, lo que buscamos
y no encontraremos nunca,
jamás!

The nest was all decked out.
A Florentine daydream
infloresced with spring,
so that in living flesh
dead longings were reborn.
Imagine an oak
that produced a fresh rose;
a good Latin aegipan
with a bacchante both Greek
and Parisian. A magnificent
music. A supreme
primitive inspiration,
full of modern things.
A vast virile pride
perfuming the *odor di femina*;
a rock throne where
a lily rests.

Divine Season! Divine
Season! Daybreak smiles
more sweetly. The tail
of the peacock exalts
its prestige. The sun heightens
its intimate influence; and the harp
of the nerves quivers alone.
O sacred Springtime!
O delight of the sacred gift
of life! O lovely palm tree
over our brows! Neck
of the swan! White dove!
Red rose! Blue pallium!
And all for you, O my soul!
And for you, body, and for you,
idea, which ties them together.
And for You, what we seek
and will never find,
not ever!

LA DULZURA DEL ÁNGELUS . . .

La dulzura del ángelus matinal y divino
que diluyen ingenuas campanas provinciales,
en un aire inocente a fuerza de rosales,
de plegaria, de ensueño de virgen y de trino

de ruiseñor, opuesto todo al rudo destino
que no cree en Dios . . . El áureo ovillo vespertino
que la tarde devana tras opacos cristales
por tejer la inconsútil tela de nuestros males

todos hechos de carne y aromados de vino . . .
Y esta atroz amargura de no gustar de nada,
de no saber a dónde dirigir nuestra prora

mientras el pobre esquife en la noche cerrada
va en las hostiles olas huérfano de la aurora . . .
(Oh, suaves campanas entre la madrugada!)

NOCTURNO

Quiero expresar mi angustia en versos que abolida
dirán mi juventud de rosas y de ensueños,
y la desfloración amarga de mi vida
por un vasto dolor y cuidados pequeños.

Y el viaje a un vago Oriente por entrevistos barcos,
y el grano de oraciones que floreció en blasfemia,
y los azoramientos del cisne entre los charcos
y el falso azul nocturno de inquerida bohemia.

Lejano clavicordio que en silencio y olvido
no diste nunca al sueño la sublime sonata,
huérfano esquife, árbol insigne, obscuro nido
que suavizó la noche de dulzura de plata . . .

THE SWEETNESS OF THE ANGELUS . . .

The sweetness of the Angelus, divine in the morning,
which ingenuous provincial bells dissolve
on a breeze made innocent by rose bushes,
prayer, virginal dreams, and the warble

of a nightingale, all opposed to the rude destiny
that doesn't believe in God . . . The golden vesper ball
which the evening spins behind opaque crystals,
weaving the seamless cloth of our ills

all made of flesh and perfumed with wine . . .
And this atrocious bitterness of not liking a thing,
of not knowing where to steer our prow

while the poor skiff in the black night
sails into hostile waves, an orphan of the dawn . . .
(O gentle bells in the early morning!)

NOCTURNE

I want to express my anguish in verses that tell
of my abolished youth of roses and daydreams,
and the bitter deflowering of my life
by a vast sorrow and petty concerns.

And the voyage to a vague Orient by ships barely glimpsed,
and the seed of prayers that flowered into blasphemy,
and the swan's befuddlement between the ponds,
and the false nocturnal blue of a detested bohemian lifestyle.

Distant harpsichord, in silence and oblivion
you never gave the sublime sonata to the dream,
orphan skiff, illustrious tree, obscure nest
which the night softened with silver sweetness . . .

Esperanza olorosa a hierbas frescas, trino
del ruiseñor primaveral y matinal,
azucena tronchada por un fatal destino,
rebusca de la dicha, persecución del mal . . .

El ánfora funesta del divino veneno
que ha de hacer por la vida la tortura interior,
la conciencia espantable de nuestro humano cieno
y el horror de sentirse pasajero, el horror

de ir a tientas, en intermitentes espantos,
hacia lo inevitable desconocido y la
pesadilla brutal de este dormir de llantos
de la cual no hay más que Ella que nos despertará!

CANCIÓN DE OTOÑO EN PRIMAVERA

A Martínez Sierra

Juventud, divino tesoro,
ya te vas para no volver!
Cuando quiero llorar, no lloro . . .
y a veces lloro sin querer . . .

Plural ha sido la celeste
historia de mi corazón.
Era una dulce niña, en este
mundo de duelo y aflicción.

Miraba como el alba pura;
sonreía como una flor.
Era su cabellera obscura
hecha de noche y de dolor.

Hope redolent with fresh herbs, a trill
from the springtime morning nightingale,
a white lily felled by a fatal destiny,
a search for happiness, a pursuit of evil . . .

The fateful amphora of the divine venom
that must bring about inner torture throughout life,
the appalling awareness of our human slime,
and the horror of feeling short-lived, the horror

of groping along, in intermittent dread,
toward the inevitable unknown and the
brutal nightmare of this weeping sleep
from which there is only She to awaken us.*

SONG OF AUTUMN IN SPRINGTIME

For Martínez Sierra

Youth, divine treasure,
you've already gone, never to return!
When I want to cry, I don't cry . . .
and sometimes I cry without wanting to . . .

Plural has been the heavenly
history of my heart.
She was a sweet child in this
world of sorrow and affliction.

She gazed like the pure dawn;
she smiled like a flower.
Her dark hair was
made of night and of pain.

---

* As in a later "Nocturne" from *El canto errante*, it must be pointed out that the noun *death* in Spanish (*la muerte*) is feminine in gender and thus requires the feminine pronoun. The conspicuous use which Darío makes of it in these poems clearly suggests his intent to personify death, and so we have opted to do the same by translating the pronoun literally.

Yo era tímido como un niño.
Ella, naturalmente, fue,
para mi amor hecho de armiño,
Herodías y Salomé . . .

Juventud, divino tesoro,
ya te vas para no volver . . . !
Cuando quiero llorar, no lloro,
y a veces lloro sin querer . . .

La otra fue más sensitiva,
y más consoladora y más
halagadora y expresiva,
cual no pensé encontrar jamás.
Pues a su continua ternura
una pasión violenta unía.
En un peplo de gasa pura
una bacante se envolvía . . .

En sus brazos tomó mi ensueño
y lo arrulló como a un bebé . . .
y le mató, triste y pequeño,
falto de luz, falto de fe . . .

Juventud, divino tesoro,
te fuiste para no volver!
Cuando quiero llorar, no lloro,
y a veces lloro sin querer . . .

Otra juzgó que era mi boca
el estuche de su pasión;
y que me roería, loca,
con sus dientes el corazón,

poniendo en un amor de exceso
la mira de su voluntad,
mientras eran abrazo y beso
síntesis de la eternidad;

I was timid as a child.
She, naturally, was,
for my love made of ermine,
Herodias and Salome . . .

Youth, divine treasure,
you've already gone, never to return . . . !
When I want to cry, I don't cry,
and sometimes I cry without wanting to . . .

The other was more susceptible,
and more comforting and more
ingratiating and affectionate,
such as I never hoped to find.
Since with her constant tenderness
she combined a violent passion.
In a peplum of pure gauze
a Bacchante was wrapped up . . .

In her hands she took my fantasy
and lulled it like a baby . . .
and she killed it, sad and small,
deprived of light, deprived of faith . . .

Youth, divine treasure,
you've already gone, never to return!
When I want to cry, I don't cry,
and sometimes I cry without wanting to . . .

Another decided that my mouth
was the sheath of her passion;
and that she would madly gnaw
my heart with her teeth,

setting on an excessive love
the sights of her determination,
while embrace and kiss were
a synthesis of eternity;

y de nuestra carne ligera
imaginar siempre un Edén,
sin pensar que la Primavera
y la carne acaban también . . .

Juventud, divino tesoro,
ya te vas para no volver!
Cuando quiero llorar, no lloro,
y a veces lloro sin querer!

Y las demás! en tantos climas,
en tantas tierras, siempre son,
si no pretextos de mis rimas,
fantasmas de mi corazón.

En vano busqué a la princesa
que estaba triste de esperar.
La vida es dura. Amarga y pesa.
Ya no hay princesa que cantar!

Mas a pesar del tiempo terco,
mi sed de amor no tiene fin;
con el cabello gris, me acerco
a los rosales del jardín . . .

Juventud, divino tesoro,
ya te vas para no volver . . .
cuando quiero llorar, no lloro,
y a veces lloro sin querer . . .

Mas es mía el Alba de oro!

DIVINA PSIQUIS, DULCE MARIPOSA INVISIBLE . . .

Divina Psiquis, dulce Mariposa invisible
que desde los abismos has venido a ser todo
lo que en mi ser nervioso y en mi cuerpo sensible
forma la chispa sacra de la estatua de lodo!

and always to picture an Eden
from our weak flesh,
not thinking that Springtime
and flesh will also end . . .

Youth, divine treasure,
you've already gone, never to return!
When I want to cry, I don't cry,
and sometimes I cry without wanting to!

And the rest of them! in so many climes,
in so many lands, they will always be,
if not pretexts for my rhymes,
phantoms of my heart.

In vain I sought the princess
who had grown sad from waiting.
Life is hard. It embitters and weighs us down.
There's no longer a princess to sing to!

Yet regardless of obstinate time,
my thirst for love has no end;
with gray hair I approach
the rosebushes of life . . .

Youth, divine treasure,
you've already gone, never to return . . .
When I want to cry, I don't cry,
and sometimes I cry without wanting to . . .

Yet the golden Dawn is mine!

DIVINE PSYCHE, SWEET INVISIBLE BUTTERFLY . . .

Divine Psyche, sweet invisible Butterfly,
you who from the depths have come to be everything
that in my nervous being and in my sensitive body
forms the sacred spark in a statue of mud!

Te asomas por mis ojos a la luz de la tierra
y prisionera vives en mí de extraño dueño:
te reducen a esclava mis sentidos en guerra
y apenas vagas libre por el jardín del sueño.

Sabia de la Lujuria que sabe antiguas ciencias,
te sacudes a veces entre imposibles muros,
y más allá de todas las vulgares conciencias
exploras los recodos más terribles y obscuros.

Y encuentras sombra y duelo. Que sombra y duelo
                              [encuentres
bajo la viña en donde nace el vino del Diablo.
Te posas en los senos, te posas en los vientres
que hicieron a Juan loco e hicieron cuerdo a Pablo.

A Juan virgen y a Pablo militar y violento,
a Juan que nunca supo del supremo contacto;
a Pablo el tempestuoso que halló a Cristo en el viento,
y a Juan ante quien Hugo se queda estupefacto.

Entre la catedral y las ruinas paganas
vuelas, ¡oh, Psiquis, oh, alma mía!
—Como decía
aquel celeste Edgardo,
que entró en el paraíso entre un son de campanas
y un perfume de nardo,—
entre la catedral
y las paganas ruinas
repartes tus dos alas de cristal,
tus dos alas divinas.
Y de la flor
que el ruiseñor
canta en su griego antiguo, de la rosa,
vuelas, ¡oh, Mariposa!
a posarte en un clavo de Nuestro Señor!

You peek out from my eyes at the light of the earth
and live as a prisoner in me, your strange master:
at war my senses reduce you to a slave
and you scarcely wander free in the garden of dreams.

Wise with the lust that knows ancient sciences,
at times you shake yourself off between impossible walls,
and beyond all the vulgar consciences
you explore the most dark and terrible twists and turns.

And you find shadow and sorrow. May you find shadow
                                        [and sorrow
under the vineyard where the Devil's wine is born.
You alight on the breasts, you alight on the wombs
that drove John crazy and drove Paul sane.

Virginal John and military, violent Paul,
John who had never learned of the supreme contact;
the tempestuous Paul who found Christ in the wind,
and John before whom Hugo is stupefied.

"Between the cathedral and the pagan ruins
you fly, O Psyche, O my soul!"
said
that heavenly Edgar,
who entered paradise with the sound of bells
and the perfume of spikenard:
between the cathedral
and the pagan ruins
you divide your two crystal wings,
your two divine wings.
And from the flower
of which the nightingale
sings in his ancient Greek, from the rose
you fly, O Butterfly!
to alight on a nail of Our Lord!

A Phocás el campesino

Phocás el campesino, hijo mío, que tienes,
en apenas escasos meses de vida tantos
dolores en tus ojos que esperan tanto llantos
por el fatal pensar que revelan tus sienes . . .

Tarda en venir a este dolor a donde vienes,
a este mundo terrible en duelos y en espantos;
duerme bajo los Angeles, sueña bajo los Santos,
que ya tendrás la Vida para que te envenenes . . .

Sueña, hijo mío, todavía, y cuando crezcas,
perdóname el fatal don de darte la vida
que yo hubiera querido de azul y rosas frescas;

pues tú eres la crisálida de mi alma entristecida,
y te he de ver en medio del triunfo que merezcas
renovando el fulgor de mi psique abolida.

Carne, celeste carne de la mujer! Arcilla . . .

Carne, celeste carne de la mujer! Arcilla,
dijo Hugo—ambrosía más bien ¡oh maravilla!
La vida se soporta,
tan doliente y tan corta,
solamente por eso:
roce, mordisco o beso
en ese pan divino
para el cual nuestra sangre es nuestro vino!
En ella está la lira,
en ella está la rosa,
en ella está la ciencia armoniosa,
en ella se respira
el perfume vital de toda cosa.

Eva y Cipris concentran el misterio
del corazón del mundo.

To Phocas the Peasant

Phocas the peasant, my son, who has had,
in the few meager months of his life, so much
pain in his eyes that expect so much weeping
for the fatal thinking which his temples reveal . . .

Take your time coming to this pain to which you'll come,
to this terrible world in sorrow and in dread;
sleep beneath the Angels, dream beneath the Saints,
you'll soon enough have Life to poison yourself with . . .

Dream on, my son, and when you grow,
forgive me the fatal gift of having given you the life
which I had wished to be all fresh roses and blue;

since you are the chrysalis of my saddened soul,
and I must see you in the midst of the triumph you deserve
renewing the splendor of my abolished psyche.

Flesh, a Woman's Heavenly Flesh! Clay . . .

Flesh, a woman's heavenly flesh. Clay,
said Hugo—rather, ambrosia. O wonder!
Life is bearable,
so painful and so short,
only because of this:
a stroke, a nibble, or a kiss
on this divine bread
for which our blood is our wine!
In it is the lyre,
in it is the rose,
in it is harmonious science,
in it we breathe
the vital perfume of each thing.

Eve and Cyprian concentrate the mystery
of the heart of the world.

Cuando el áureo Pegaso
en la victoria matinal se lanza
con el mágico ritmo de su paso
hacia la vida y hacia la esperanza,
si alza la crin y las narices hincha
y sobre las montañas pone el casco sonoro
y hacia la mar relincha,
y el espacio se llena
de un gran temblor de oro,
es que ha visto desnuda a Anadiomena.

Gloria, ¡oh, Potente a quien las sombras temen!
Que las más blancas tórtolas te inmolen!
Pues por ti la floresta está en el polen
y el pensamiento en el sagrado semen!
Gloria, ¡oh, Sublime que eres la existencia,
por quien siempre hay futuros en el útero eterno!
Tu boca sabe al fruto del árbol de la Ciencia
y al torcer tus cabellos apagaste el infierno!

Inútil es el grito de la legión cobarde
del interés, inútil el progreso
yankee, si te desdeña.
Si el progreso es de fuego, por ti arde,
toda lucha del hombre va a tu beso,
por ti se combate o se sueña!

Pues en ti existe Primavera para el triste,
labor gozosa para el fuerte,
néctar, Anfora, dulzura amable.
Porque en ti existe
el placer de vivir, hasta la muerte—
y ante la eternidad de lo probable . . . !

Cleopompo y Heliodemo

Cleopompo y Heliodemo, cuya filosofía
es idéntica, gustan dialogar bajo el verde

When golden Pegasus
in the morning victory hurtles upward
with the magical rhythm of his passage
toward life and toward hope,
if he raises his mane and flares his nostrils
and over the mountains sets his sonorous hoof
and snorts toward the sea,
and space is filled
with a great quaking of gold,
it is because he has seen Anadyomene naked.

Glory, O Mighty One whom the shadows fear!
May the whitest turtledoves immolate you!
Since because of you the forest is in the pollen
and thought in the sacred semen!
Glory, O Sublime One who is existence,
because of whom there are always futures in the eternal uterus!
Your mouth tastes of the fruit of the Tree of Knowledge,
and when you wrung out your hair you extinguished hell!

Useless is the shout of the cowardly legion
of profit, useless Yankee
progress, if it disdains you.
If progress is made of fire, for you it burns,
every struggle of man moves toward your kiss,
because of you there is combat or there is dreaming!

For in you does Springtime exist for the sad,
joyful labor for the strong,
nectar, Amphora, amiable sweetness.
Because in you
the pleasure of living exists, until death—
and face to face with the eternity of the probable . . . !

CLEOPOMPUS AND HELIODEMOS

Cleopompus and Heliodemos, whose philosophy
is identical, like to confer under the green

palio del platanar. Allí Cleopompo muerde
la manzana epicúrea y Heliodemo fía

al aire su confianza en la eterna armonía.
Mal haya quien las Parcas inhumano recuerde:
si una sonora perla de la clepsidra pierde,
no volverá a ofrecerla la mano que la envía.

Una vaca aparece, crepuscular. Es hora
en que el grillo en su lira hace halagos a Flora,
y en el azul florece un diamante supremo:

y en la pupila enorme de la bestia apacible
miran como que rueda en un ritmo visible
la música del mundo, Cleopompo y Heliodemo.

DE OTOÑO

Yo sé que hay quienes dicen: ¿Por qué no canta ahora
con aquella locura armoniosa de antaño?
Esos no ven la obra profunda de la hora,
la labor del minuto y el prodigio del año.

Yo, pobre árbol, produje, al amor de la brisa,
cuando empecé a crecer, un vago y dulce son.
Pasó ya el tiempo de la juvenil sonrisa:
dejad al huracán mover mi corazón!

NOCTURNO

A Mariano de Cavia

Los que auscultasteis el corazón de la noche,
los que por el insomnio tenaz habéis oído
el cerrar de una puerta, el resonar de un coche
lejano, un eco vago, un ligero ruido . . .

pallium of the banana plantation. There Cleopompus bites
the Epicurean apple and Heliodemos entrusts

to the breeze his confidence in eternal harmony.
Woe unto him who, inhumane, tempts the Fates:
if a sonorous pearl drops through the clepsydra,
the hand which sent it will not offer it again.

A cow appears, like twilight. It's the time
when the cricket on his lyre makes sweet-talk to Flora,
and in the blue a supreme diamond blooms:

and in the enormous pupil of the placid beast,
Cleopompus and Heliodemos watch the music of the world
rolling in a visible rhythm.

IN AUTUMN

I know that there are those who say, "Why don't you sing now
with that harmonious madness of old?"
They don't see the profound work of an hour,
the labor of a minute, and the prodigy of a year.

I, a poor tree, produced, out of love for the breeze,
when I began to grow, a vague and sweet sound.
The time for youthful smiles has long passed:
Let the hurricane move my heart!

NOCTURNE

For Mariano de Cavia

Those of you who auscultated the heart of the night,
who with tenacious insomnia have heard
the closing of a door, the rumble of a car
in the distance, a vague echo, a soft noise . . .

En los instantes del silencio misterioso,
cuando surgen de su prisión los olvidados,
en la hora de los muertos, en la hora del reposo,
sabréis leer estos versos de amargor impregnados . . . !

Como en un vaso vierto en ellos mis dolores
de lejanos recuerdos y desgracias funestas,
y las tristes nostalgias de mi alma, ebria de flores,
y el duelo de mi corazón, triste de fiestas.

Y el pesar de no ser lo que yo hubiera sido,
la pérdida del reino que estaba para mí,
el pensar que un instante pude no haber nacido,
y el sueño que es mi vida desde que yo nací!

Todo esto viene en medio del silencio profundo
en que la noche envuelve la terrena ilusión,
y siento como un eco del corazón del mundo
que penetra y conmueve mi propio corazón.

LO FATAL

A René Pérez

Dichoso el árbol que es apenas sensitivo,
y más la piedra dura porque ésa ya no siente,
pues no hay dolor más grande que el dolor de ser vivo,
ni mayor pesadumbre que la vida consciente.

Ser, y no saber nada, y ser sin rumbo cierto,
y el temor de haber sido y un futuro terror . . .
Y el espanto seguro de estar mañana muerto,
y sufrir por la vida y por la sombra y por

lo que no conocemos y apenas sospechamos,
y la carne que tienta con sus frescos racimos,
y la tumba que aguarda con sus fúnebres ramos,
y no saber a dónde vamos,
ni de dónde venimos . . . !

In moments of mysterious silence,
when the forgotten emerge from their prison,
at the hour of the dead, at the hour of repose,
you'll know how to read these verses steeped in bitterness . . . !

As into a glass I pour into them my sorrows
from distant memories and fateful misfortunes,
and the sad nostalgias of my soul, drunk on flowers,
and the grief of my heart, saddened by parties.

And the regret of not being what I might have been,
the loss of the kingdom that was to be mine,
the thought that for just an instant I could have not been born,
and the dream that is my life ever since I was born!

All this comes in the midst of profound silence
when the night envelops earthly hope,
and I feel like an echo from the heart of the world
that penetrates and moves my own heart.

What Gets You

For René Pérez

How fortunate the tree that is scarcely aware,
and more so the hard stone because it no longer feels,
since there is no greater pain than the pain of living,
nor deeper sorrow than conscious life.

Being, and knowing nothing, and being without a true course,
and the fear of having been, and a future terror . . .
And the certain dread of being dead tomorrow,
and suffering because of life, and because of shadow, and because of

what we don't know and scarcely suspect,
and the flesh that tempts with its fresh-picked bunches,
and the tomb that awaits with its funeral bouquets,
and not knowing where we are going,
nor from where we have come . . . !

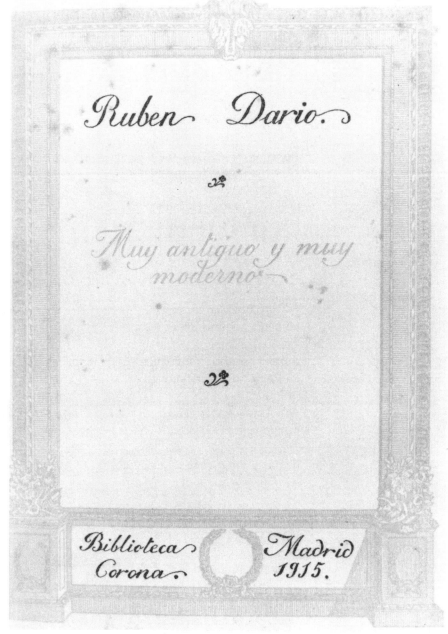

Ruben Dario.

Muy antiguo y muy
moderno

Biblioteca   Madrid
Corona   1915.

Muy antiguo y muy moderno was the title of one of the volumes of Darío's final personal anthology. Published a year before his death, this volume offers an insight into the poet's vision and selection of his own poetry.

EL CANTO ERRANTE
(1907)

EL CANTOR VA POR TODO EL MUNDO . . .

El cantor va por todo el mundo
sonriente o meditabundo.

El cantor va sobre la tierra
en blanca paz o en roja guerra.

Sobre el lomo del elefante
por la enorme India alucinante.

En palanquín y en seda fina
por el corazón de la China;

en automóvil en Lutecia;
en negra góndola en Venecia;

sobre las pampas y los llanos
en los potros americanos;

por el río va en la canoa,
o se le ve sobre la proa

de un steamer sobre el vasto mar,
o en un wagón de sleeping-car.

El dromedario del desierto,
barco vivo, le lleva a un puerto.

Sobre el raudo trineo trepa
en la blancura de la estepa.

O en el silencio de cristal
que ama la aurora boreal.

200

THE ROVING SONG
(1907)

THE SINGER GOES ALL OVER THE WORLD . . .

The singer goes all over the world
smiling or thoughtful.

The singer roams the earth
in white peace or in red war.

On the back of an elephant
through enormous, hallucinatory India.

On a palanquin and in fine silk
through the heart of China;

in a car in Lutetia;
in a black gondola in Venice;

over the prairies and the plains
on American colts;

by river he goes in a canoe,
or he is seen at the prow

of a steamer on the vast sea,
or in a sleeping car.

The dromedary of the desert,
a living ship, carries him into port.

In a swift sled he scales
the whiteness of the steppe.

Or the crystal silence
which the Northern Lights love.

El cantor va a pie por los prados,
entre las siembras y ganados.

Y entra en su Londres en el tren,
y en asno a su Jerusalén.

Con estafetas y con malas,
va el cantor por la humanidad.

El cantor vuela, con sus alas:
Armonía y Eternidad.

Metempsícosis

Yo fui un soldado que durmió en el lecho
de Cleopatra la reina. Su blancura
y su mirada astral y omnipotente.
                    Eso fue todo.

Oh mirada! oh blancura! y oh aquel lecho
en que estaba radiante la blancura!
Oh la rosa marmórea omnipotente!
Eso fue todo.

Y crujió su espinazo por mi brazo;
y yo, liberto, hice olvidar a Antonio,
(oh el lecho y la mirada y la blancura!)
                    Eso fue todo.

Yo, Rufo Galo, fui soldado, y sangre
tuve de Galia, y la imperial becerra
me dio un minuto audaz de su capricho.
                    Eso fue todo.

Por qué en aquel espasmo las tenazas
de mis dedos de bronce no apretaron
el cuello de la blanca reina en brama?
                    Eso fue todo.

The singer walks through meadows,
among the crops and the livestock.

And enters his London by train,
and atop an ass his Jerusalem.

With diplomatic pouches and with mailbags
the singer goes for humanity.

The singer flies, with his wings:
Harmony and Eternity.

METEMPSYCHOSIS

I was a soldier who slept in the bed
of Cleopatra the queen. Her whiteness
and her astral, omnipotent gaze.
          That is all over.

O gaze! O whiteness! and O that bed
where her whiteness seemed radiant!
O the marmoreal, omnipotent rose!
          That is all over.

And her backbone cracked in my arms;
and I, emancipated, made her forget Antony.
(O the bed and the gaze and the whiteness!)
          That is all over.

I, Rufus Gallus, was a soldier, and bore
the blood of Gaul, and the imperial heifer
gave me one brazen minute of her fancy.
          That is all over.

Why in that spasm did the pincers
of my bronze fingers not squeeze
the neck of the white queen in rut?
          That is all over.

Yo fui llevado a Egipto. La cadena
tuve al pescuezo. Fui comido un día
por los perros. Mi nombre, Rufo Galo.
　　　　Eso fue todo.

VERSOS DE OTOÑO

Cuando mi pensamiento va hacia ti, se perfuma;
tu mirar es tan dulce, que se torna profundo.
Bajo tus pies desnudos aún hay blancor de espuma,
y en tus labios compendias la alegría del mundo.

El amor pasajero tiene el encanto breve,
y ofrece un igual término para el gozo y la pena.
Hace una hora que un nombre grabé sobre la nieve;
hace un minuto dije mi amor sobre la arena.

Las hojas amarillas caen en la alameda,
en donde vagan tantas parejas amorosas.
Y en la copa de Otoño un vago vino queda
en que han de deshojarse, Primavera, tus rosas.

SUM . . .

Yo soy en Dios lo que soy
y mi ser es voluntad
que, perseverando hoy,
existe en la eternidad.

Cuatro horizontes de abismo
tiene mi razonamiento,
y el abismo que más siento
es el que siento en mí mismo.

Hay un punto alucinante
en mi villa de ilusión:

I was brought to Egypt. A chain
hung around my neck. I was eaten one day
by dogs. My name, Rufus Gallus.
                    That is all over.

AUTUMN VERSES

When my thought strays to you, it becomes perfumed;
your glance is so sweet, it turns profound.
Under your naked feet there is still the whiteness of foam,
and in your lips you epitomize the joy of the world.

Short-lived love has a brief charm
and offers the same end to delight and sorrow.
An hour ago I engraved a name in the snow;
a minute ago I expressed my love on the sand.

Yellow leaves fall on the boulevard
where so many loving couples stroll.
And in Autumn's cup there is a vague wine
into which your roses, Springtime, will drop their petals.

SUM . . .

I am in God what I am
and my being is a will
that, persevering today,
exists in eternity.

My reasoning has
four horizons of an abyss,
and the abyss I feel the most
is the one I feel within me.

There is a hallucinatory point
in my villa of hope:

la torre del elefante
junto al kiosco del pavón.

Aún lo humilde me subyuga
si lo dora mi deseo.
La concha de la tortuga
me dice el dolor de Orfeo.

Rosas buenas, lirios pulcros,
loco de tanto ignorar,
voy a ponerme a gritar
al borde de los sepulcros:

Señor que la fe se muere!
Señor mira mi dolor.
Miserere! Miserere! . . .
Dame la mano, Señor . . .

EHEU!

Aquí, junto al mar latino,
digo la verdad:
siento en roca, aceite y vino
yo mi antigüedad.

Oh, qué anciano soy, Dios santo,
oh, qué anciano soy . . .
¿De dónde viene mi canto?
Y yo, ¿adónde voy?

El conocerme a mí mismo
ya me va costando
muchos momentos de abismo
y el cómo y el cuándo . . .

Y esta claridad latina,
¿de qué me sirvió

the elephant's tower
beside the peacock's pavilion.

Still the humble overpowers me
if my desire gilds it.
The shell of the turtle
tells me the pain of Orpheus.

Virtuous roses, spotless lilies—
mad from not knowing so much
I am going to start shouting
at the edge of the sepulchers:

Lord, my faith is dying!
Lord, look upon my pain.
Miserere! Miserere! . . .
Stretch forth Thy hand, Lord . . .

EHEU!

Here, by the Latin sea,
I will speak the truth:
I feel in a rock, oil, and wine
my own antiquity.

Oh, what an old man I am, dear God,
oh, what an old man I am . . .
Where does my song come from?
And I, where am I going?

Knowing myself
is now beginning to cost me
many abysmal moments
and the how and the when . . .

And this Latin clarity,
what good did it do me

a la entrada de la mina
del yo y el no yo . . . ?

Nefelibata contento
creo interpretar
las confidencias del viento,
la tierra y el mar . . .

Unas vagas confidencias
del ser y el no ser,
y fragmentos de conciencias
de ahora y ayer.

Como en medio de un desierto
me puse a clamar;
y miré el sol como muerto
y me eché a llorar.

NOCTURNO

Silencio de la noche, doloroso silencio
nocturno . . . ¿Por qué el alma tiembla de tal manera?
Oigo el zumbido de mi sangre,
dentro mi cráneo pasa una suave tormenta.
Insomnio! No poder dormir, y, sin embargo,
soñar. Ser la auto-pieza
de disección espiritual, el auto-Hamlet!
Diluir mi tristeza
en un vino de noche
en el maravilloso cristal de las tinieblas . . .
Y me digo: ¿a qué hora vendrá el alba?
Se ha cerrado una puerta . . .
Ha pasado un transeúnte . . .
Ha dado el reloj trece horas . . . Si será Ella! . . .

at the entrance to the mine
of self and not self . . . ?

A cheerful Nephelibata
I think that I can interpret
the confidences of the wind,
the earth, and the sea . . .

Some vague confidences
of being and not being,
and fragments of an awareness
of now and of yesterday.

As if in the middle of a desert,
I began to cry out;
and I looked at the sun as a dead thing
and I burst into tears.

NOCTURNE

Silence of the night, a sorrowful silence,
nocturnal . . . Why does the soul tremble like this?
I hear the hum of my blood,
in my cranium a soft storm passes.
Insomnia! Not being able to sleep, and yet
dreaming. Being the self-specimen
of spiritual dissection, the self-Hamlet!
Watering down my sadness
in a wine of night,
in the marvelous crystal of darkness . . .
And I say to myself: What time will the dawn come?
A door has shut . . .
Someone has passed on foot . . .
The clock has struck thirteen . . . But this must be She!*

---

*As in a previous "Nocturne" from *Cantos de vida y esperanza*, it must be pointed out that the noun *death* in Spanish (*la muerte*) is feminine in gender, and that Darío uses the feminine pronoun to personify death.

BALADA EN HONOR DE LAS MUSAS DE CARNE Y HUESO

A G. Martínez Sierra

Nada mejor para cantar la vida,
y aun para dar sonrisas a la muerte,
que la áurea copa en donde Venus vierte
la esencia azul de su viña encendida.
Por respirar los perfumes de Armida
y por sorber el vino de su beso,
vino de ardor, de beso, de embeleso,
fuérase al cielo en la bestia de Orlando,
¡voz de oro y miel para decir cantando:
la mejor musa es la de carne y hueso!

Cabellos largos en la buhardilla,
noches de insomnio al blancor del invierno,
pan de dolor con la sal de lo eterno
y ojos de ardor en que Juvencia brilla;
el tiempo en vano mueve su cuchilla,
el hilo de oro permanece ileso;
visión de gloria para el libro impreso
que en sueños va como una mariposa;
y una esperanza en la boca de rosa:
¡la mejor musa es la de carne y hueso!

Regio automóvil, regia cetrería,
borla y muceta, heráldica fortuna,
nada son como a la luz de la luna
una mujer hecha una melodía.
Barca de amar busca la fantasía,
no el yacht de Alfonso o la barca de Creso.
Da al cuerpo llama y fortifica el seso
ese archivado y vital paraíso;
pasad de largo, Abelardo y Narciso:
¡la mejor musa es la de carne y hueso!

Clío está en esta frente hecha de aurora,
Euterpe canta en esta lengua fina,

BALLAD IN HONOR OF THE MUSES OF FLESH AND BLOOD

For G. Martínez Sierra

Nothing better for singing of life,
and even for smiling at death,
than the golden cup where Venus pours
the blue essence of her flaming wine.
For breathing the perfumes of Armida
and for sipping the wine of her kiss,
wine of an ardor, of a kiss, of a bewitchment,
one should take to the sky on Orlando's beast—
voice of gold and honey for speaking in song:
the best muse is made of flesh and blood!

Long tresses in the garret,
nights of insomnia in the white of winter,
bread of pain with the salt of the eternal,
and eyes of ardor where Juventia shines;
time in vain swings its blade,
the golden thread remains unscathed;
a vision of glory for the printed book
that in dreams moves like a butterfly;
and a hope in the mouth of a rose:
the best muse is made of flesh and blood!

Regal automobile, regal falconry,
hood and tassel, heraldic fortune,
are nothing like, in the light of the moon,
a woman made from a melody.
A ship of love-making seeks fantasy,
not the yacht of Alfonso or the ship of Croesus.
That vital paradise on the shelf
gives a flame to the body and fortifies the brains;
Just walk on by, Abelard and Narcissus:
the best muse is made of flesh and blood!

Clio is in this forehead made of dawn,
Euterpe sings in this fine tongue,

Talía ríe en la boca divina,
Melpómene es ese gesto que implora;
en estos pies Terpsícore se adora,
cuello inclinado es de Erato embeleso,
Polymnia intenta a Calíope proceso
por esos ojos en que Amor se quema.
Urania rige todo ese sistema:
¡la mejor musa es la de carne y hueso!

No protestéis con celo protestante,
contra el panal de rosas y claveles
en que Tiziano moja sus pinceles
y gusta el cielo de Beatrice el Dante.
Por eso existe el verso de diamante,
por eso el iris tiéndese y por eso
humano genio es celeste progreso.
Líricos cantan y meditan sabios
por esos pechos y por esos labios:
¡la mejor musa es la de carne y hueso!

Envío:
Gregorio: nada al cantor determina
como el gentil estímulo del beso;
gloria al sabor de la boca divina:
¡la mejor musa es la de carne y hueso!

Thalia laughs in this divine mouth,
Melpomene is that look which implores;
on these feet Terpsichore is adored,
a bowing neck is Erato's enchantment,
Polyhymnia brings a complaint against Calliope
for those eyes where Love burns.
Urania rules that whole system:
the best muse is made of flesh and blood!

Do not protest with a Protestant zeal
against the honeycomb of roses and carnations
where Titian dips his brushes
and Dante enjoys the heaven of Beatrice.
This is why the diamond verse exists,
this is why the rainbow spreads out and why
human genius is heavenly progress.
Sages meditate and the lyrical sing
for those breasts and those eyes:
the best muse is made of flesh and blood!

ENVOY:
Gregorio: nothing gives the singer more resolve
than the gentle incentive of a kiss;
glory to the taste of the divine mouth:
the best muse is made of flesh and blood!

Rubén Darío, Secretary of the Nicaraguan Committee sent to Spain to celebrate the Fourth Centennial of the Discovery of America, in 1892.

POEMA DEL OTOÑO

Tú, que estás la barba en la mano
meditabundo,
¿has dejado pasar, hermano,
la flor del mundo?

Te lamentas de los ayeres
con quejas vanas:
¡aún hay promesas de placeres
en los mañanas!

Aún puedes casar la olorosa
rosa y el lis,
y hay mirtos para tu orgullosa
cabeza gris.

El alma ahíta cruel inmola
lo que la alegra,
como Zingua, reina de Angola,
lúbrica negra.

Tú has gozado de la hora amable,
y oyes después
la imprecación del formidable
Eclesiastés.

El domingo de amor te hechiza;
mas mira cómo
llega el miércoles de ceniza:
Memento, homo . . .

Por eso hacia el florido monte
las almas van,
y se explican Anacreonte
y Omar Kayam.

216

THE AUTUMN POEM

You, there with your chin in hand,
thoughtful;
brother, have you allowed
the flower of the world to pass you by?

You cry over your yesterdays
with vain complaints:
there are still promises of pleasure
in your tomorrows!

Even now you can wed the redolent
rose to the lily,
and there are myrtles for your proud
gray head.

Your cruel and jaded soul immolates
what makes it happy,
like Zingua, queen of Angola,
a lubricious black woman.

You have enjoyed the sweet hour,
and afterwards hear
the imprecation of formidable
Ecclesiastes.

The Sunday of love bewitched you;
yet see how
Ash Wednesday is coming:
Memento, homo . . .

This is why to the flowery mount
souls go,
and why Anacreon
and Omar Khayyam express themselves.

Huyendo del mal, de improviso
se entra en el mal
por la puerta del paraíso
artificial.

Y, no obstante, la vida es bella,
por poseer
la perla, la rosa, la estrella
y la mujer.

Lucifer brilla. Canta el ronco
mar. Y se pierde
Silvano oculto tras el tronco
del haya verde.

Y sentimos la vida pura,
clara, real,
cuando la envuelve la dulzura
primaveral.

¿Para qué las envidias viles
y las injurias,
cuando retuercen sus reptiles
pálidas furias?

¿Para qué los odios funestos
de los ingratos?

¿Para qué los lívidos gestos
de los Pilatos?

¡Si lo terreno acaba, en suma,
cielo e infierno,
y nuestras vidas son la espuma
de un mar eterno!

Lavemos bien de nuestra veste
la amarga prosa;

Fleeing from evil, unexpectedly
one enters evil
through the door of a paradise
that is artificial.

And, nevertheless, life is beautiful
because it possesses
the pearl, the rose, the star,
and woman.

Lucifer shines. The hoarse sea
sings. And the secretive Sylvanus
disappears behind the trunk
of a green beech.

And we sense life pure,
clear, real,
when springtime sweetness
envelops it.

What is the use of vile envies
and offenses,
when their reptiles tightly coil around
pale rages?

What is the use of the dismal hatreds
of ingrates?

What is the use of the livid expressions
of Pilates?

If what is earthly finishes, in short,
heaven and hell,
and our lives are the foam
of an eternal sea!

Let's wash our vestment clean
of bitter prose;

soñemos en una celeste,
mística rosa.

Cojamos la flor del instante;
¡la melodía
de la mágica alondra cante
la miel del día!

Amor a su fiesta convida
y nos corona.
Todos tenemos en la vida
nuestra Verona.

Aun en la hora crepuscular
canta una voz:
«¡Ruth, risueña, viene a espigar
para Booz!»

Mas coged la flor del instante,
cuando en Oriente
nace el alba para el fragante
adolescente.

¡Oh! Niña que con Eros juegas,
niños lozanos,
danzad como las ninfas griegas
y los silvanos.

El viejo tiempo todo roe
y va deprisa;
sabed vencerle, Cintia, Cloe
y Cidalisa.

Trocad por rosas azahares,
que suena el son
de aquel Cantar de los Cantares
de Salomón.

let's dream of a celestial,
mystical rose.

Let's pick the flower of the moment;
may the melody
of the magical skylark sing
the honey of the day!

Love invites us to its feast
and crowns us.
All of us have in life
our Verona.

Still in the twilight hour
a voice is singing:
"Ruth, smiling, comes to glean
for Boaz!"

Yet pick the flower of the moment,
when in the Orient
dawn is born for the fragrant
adolescent boy.

Oh! Girl playing with Eros,
vigorous boys,
dance like Greek nymphs
and sylvans.

Father Time nibbles everything
and scurries off;
know how to overcome him, Cynthia, Chloe,
and Cydalisa.

Swap orange blossoms for roses,
for a sound will resonate
of that *Song of Songs*
of Solomon.

Príapo vela en los jardines
que Cipris huella;
Hécate hace aullar los mastines;
mas Diana es bella,

y apenas envuelta en los velos
de la ilusión,
baja a los bosques de los cielos
por Endimión.

¡Adolescencia! Amor te dora
con su virtud;
goza del beso de la aurora,
¡oh juventud!

¡Desventurado el que ha cogido
tarde la flor!
Y ¡ay de aquel que nunca ha sabido
lo que es amor!

Yo he visto en tierra tropical
la sangre arder,
como en un cáliz de cristal,
en la mujer.

Y en todas partes la que ama
y se consume
como una flor hecha de llama
y de perfume.

Abrasaos en esa llama
y respirad
ese perfume que embalsama
la Humanidad.

Gozad de la carne, ese bien
que hoy nos hechiza,
y después se tornará en
polvo y ceniza.

Priapus keeps watch in the gardens
where the Cyprian treads;
Hecate makes the mastiffs howl;
yet Diana is beautiful,

and thinly swathed in the veils
of illusion,
descends to the woods from the heavens
for Endymion.

Adolescence! Love gilds you
with its virtue;
enjoy the kiss of the dawn,
O time of youth!

Pity the poor man who has picked
the flower too late!
And alas for him who has never known
what love is!

I have seen in a tropical land
blood burning,
as if in a crystal chalice,
in a woman.

And everywhere the woman who loves
and is consumed
like a flower made of flame
and of perfume.

Burn in that flame
and breathe
that perfume which soothes
Humanity.

Enjoy the flesh, that good
which today enchants us,
and afterwards turns into
dust and ashes.

Gozad del sol, de la pagana
luz de sus fuegos;
gozad del sol, porque mañana
estaréis ciegos.

Gozad de la dulce armonía
que a Apolo invoca;
gozad del canto, porque un día
no tendréis boca.

Gozad de la tierra, que un
bien cierto encierra;
gozad, porque no estáis aún
bajo la tierra.

Apartad el temor que os hiela
y que os restringe;
la paloma de Venus vuela
sobre la Esfinge.

Aún vencen muerte, tiempo y hado
las amorosas;
en las tumbas se han encontrado
mirtos y rosas.

Aún Anadiómena en sus lidias
nos da su ayuda;
aún resurge en la obra de Fidias
Friné desnuda.

Vive el bíblico Adán robusto,
de sangre humana,
y aún siente nuestra lengua el gusto
de la manzana.

Y hace de este globo viviente
fuerza y acción
la universal y omnipotente
fecundación.

Enjoy the sun, the pagan
light of its fires;
enjoy the sun, because tomorrow
you will be blind.

Enjoy the sweet harmony
that invokes Apollo;
enjoy the song, because one day
you will have no mouth.

Enjoy the earth in which a
sure benefit is enclosed;
enjoy, because you are not yet
under the earth.

Disregard the dread that chills you
and cramps you;
the dove of Venus flies
over the Sphinx.

Still overcoming death, time, and fate
are the amorous women;
on their graves have been found
myrtles and roses.

Still Anadyomene in her battles
gives us her aid;
still in the works of Phidias
Phryne emerges naked.

The sturdy biblical Adam,
of human blood, is living,
and our tongue still perceives the taste
of the apple.

And universal and omnipotent
fertilization
makes from this living globe
force and action.

El corazón del cielo late
por la victoria
de este vivir, que es un combate
y es una gloria.

Pues aunque hay pena y nos agravia
el sino adverso,
en nosotros corre la savia
del universo.

Nuestro cráneo guarda el vibrar
de tierra y sol,
como el ruido de la mar
el caracol.

La sal del mar en nuestras venas
va a borbotones;
tenemos sangre de sirenas
y de tritones.

A nosotros encinas, lauros,
frondas espesas:
tenemos carne de centauros
y satiresas.

En nosotros la Vida vierte
fuerza y calor.
¡Vamos al reino de la Muerte
por el camino del Amor!

The heart of the sky throbs
for the victory
of this living, which is a combat
and a glory.

Now although there is woe, and adverse fate
plagues us,
in us runs the sap
of the universe.

Our cranium holds the vibrating
of earth and sun,
as the sound of the sea
the seashell.

The salt of the sea in our veins
bubbles up;
we have the blood of mermaids
and of tritons.

In us oak leaves, laurels,
dense fronds;
we have the flesh of centaurs
and satyresses.

Into us Life pours
force and heat.
Let's go to the realm of Death
on the road of Love!

Letter from Rubén Darío to the poet Juan Ramón Jiménez, sent while on a trip to Morocco.

La Cartuja

Este vetusto monasterio ha visto,
secos de orar y pálidos de ayuno,
con el breviario y con el Santo Cristo,
a los callados hijos de San Bruno.

A los que en su existencia solitaria,
con la locura de la cruz y al vuelo
místicamente azul de la plegaria,
fueron a Dios en busca de consuelo.

Mortificaron con las disciplinas
y los cilicios la carne mortal
y opusieron, orando, las divinas
ansias celestes al furor sexual.

La soledad que amaba Jeremías,
el misterioso profesor de llanto,
y el silencio, en que encuentran armonías
el soñador, el místico y el santo,

fueron para ellos minas de diamantes
que cavan los mineros serafines
a la luz de los cirios parpadeantes
y al son de las campanas de maitines.

Gustaron las harinas celestiales
en el maravilloso simulacro,
herido el cuerpo bajo los sayales,
el espíritu ardiente en amor sacro.

Vieron la nada amarga de este mundo,
pozos de horror y dolores extremos,
y hallaron el concepto más profundo
en el profundo «De morir tenemos».

SONG TO ARGENTINA AND OTHER POEMS
(1914)

THE CHARTERHOUSE

This old monastery has seen,
dried-up from praying and pale from fasting,
with the breviary and with the Holy Christ,
the silent sons of St. Bruno.

Those who in their solitary existence,
with madness for the cross and in the flight
—mystically blue—of prayer,
went to God in search of comfort.

They mortified with disciplines
and hair shirts their mortal flesh,
and their divine heavenly yearnings
resisted, through prayer, their sexual furor.

The solitude loved by Jeremiah,
that mysterious master of weeping,
and the silence, where harmonies are found
by the dreamer, the mystic, and the saint,

were for them diamond mines
where the seraphim miners dig
by the light of flickering candles
and the sound of the bells to matins.

The heavenly flour pleased them
in the marvelous simulacrum,
the body bruised beneath the sackcloth,
the spirit burning in sacred love.

They saw the bitter nothingness of this world,
wells of horror and excessive pain,
and came across the most profound concept
in the profound "*We have to die.*"

Y como a Pablo e Hilarión y Antonio,
a pesar de cilicios y oraciones,
les presentó, con su hechizo, el demonio
sus mil visiones de fornicaciones.

Y fueron castos por dolor y fe,
y fueron pobres por la santidad,
y fueron obedientes porque fue
su reina de pies blancos la humildad.

Vieron los belcebúes y satanes
que esas almas humildes y apostólicas
triunfaban de maléficos afanes
y de tantas acedias melancólicas.

Que el *Mortui estis* del candente Pablo
les forjaba corazas arcangélicas
y que nada podría hacer el diablo
de halagos finos o añagazas bélicas.

¡Ah! fuera yo de esos que Dios quería,
y que Dios quiere cuando así le place,
dichosos ante el temeroso día
de losa fría y ¡*Requiescat in pace!*

Poder matar el orgullo perverso
y el palpitar de la carne maligna,
todo por Dios, delante el Universo,
con corazón que sufre y se resigna.

Sentir la unción de la divina mano,
ver florecer de eterna luz mi anhelo,
y oír como un Pitágoras cristiano
la música teológica del cielo.

Y al fauno que hay en mí, darle la ciencia
que al Angel hace estremecer las alas.
Por la oración y por la penitencia
poner en fuga a las diablesas malas.

And as to Paul and Hilarion and Anthony,
in spite of hair shirts and prayers,
the devil, with his sorcery, presented to them
his thousand visions of fornication.

And they were chaste because of pain and faith,
and they were poor because of sanctity,
and they were obedient because their queen
with white feet was humility.

The beelzebubs and satans saw
that those humble and apostolic souls
would triumph over baleful urges
and many melancholy discouragements.

Because the *Mortui estis* of candescent Paul
forged for them archangelic cuirasses
and because the devil could do nothing
with smooth words or bellicose bluffs.

Oh, if only I were one of those whom God loved,
and whom God loves for pleasing him,
those blissful as they face the fearful day
of a cold slab and *Requiescat in pace!*

To be able to slay perverse pride
and the throbbing of malignant flesh,
all for God, before the Universe,
with a heart that suffers and submits.

To feel the anointing of the divine hand,
to see my longings blossom into eternal light,
and to hear like a Christian Pythagoras
the theological music of the heavens.

And to give the faun there is in me, the science
that makes the Angel flutter his wings.
Through prayer and through penitence
to put to flight the wicked female devils.

Darme otros ojos, no estos ojos vivos
que gozan en mirar, como los ojos
de los sátiros locos medio-chivos,
redondeces de nieve y labios rojos.

Darme otra boca en que queden impresos
los ardientes carbones del asceta,
y no esta boca en que vinos y besos
aumentan gulas de hombre y de poeta.

Darme unas manos de disciplinante
que me dejen el lomo ensangrentado,
y no estas manos lúbricas de amante
que acarician las pomas del pecado.

Darme una sangre que me deje llenas
las venas de quietud y en paz los sesos,
y no esta sangre que hace arder las venas,
vibrar los nervios y crujir los huesos.

¡Y quedar libre de maldad y engaño,
y sentir una mano que me empuja
a la cueva que acoge al ermitaño,
o al silencio y la paz de la Cartuja!

GESTA DEL COSO

Dramatis Personae

El Toro, El Buey, la Muchedumbre

América. Un coso. La tarde. El sol brilla radiosamente en un cielo despejado. En el anfiteatro hay un inmenso número de espectadores. En la arena, después de la muerte de varios toros, la cuadrilla se prepara para retirarse triunfante. El primer beluario, cerca de una huella sangrienta, está gallardo, vestido de azul y oro, muleta y espada bajo el brazo. Los banderilleros visten de amarillo y plata. En las chaquetas de los picadores espejean las lentejuelas al resplandor de la tarde. En el toril han quedado: un toro, hermoso y bravo, y un buey de servicio. Son de clarín.

To give myself other eyes, not these living eyes
that enjoy watching—like the eyes
of mad satyrs who are half-goat—
curvatures of snow and red lips.

To give myself another mouth stamped
with the burning coals of the ascetic,
and not this mouth where wines and kisses
increase the gluttony of man and of poet.

To give myself a pair of flagellant's hands
that leave my back bloody,
and not these lewd lover's hands
that caress the apples of sin.

To give myself a blood that leaves my veins
full of quiet and my brains at peace,
and not this blood that makes the veins burn,
the nerves quiver, and the bones gnash.

And to be free of wickedness and deceit,
and to feel a hand impelling me
into a cave that welcomes the hermit,
or into the silence and peace of the Charterhouse!

EXPLOIT IN THE BULLRING

Dramatis Personae

The Bull, the Ox, the Crowd

America. A bullring. Afternoon. The sun shines radiantly in a cloudless sky.
In the amphitheater there is an immense number of spectators. In the arena,
after the death of several bulls, the *cuadrilla* team prepares to depart trium-
phant. The first man, near a bloody track, is elegant, dressed in blue and
gold, a *muleta* and sword under his arm. The *banderilleros* are dressed in
yellow and silver. Sequins shimmer on the jackets of the picadors in the
afternoon glare. In the bullpen are: a bull, handsome and brave, and a work
ox. The sound of a bugle.

LA MUCHEDUMBRE
¡Otro toro! ¡Otro toro!

EL BUEY
¿Has escuchado?
Prepara empuje, cuernos y pellejo:
ha llegado tu turno. Ira salvaje,
banderillas y picas que te acosan,
aplausos al verdugo; al fin, la muerte.
Y arriba, la impasible y solitaria
contemplación del vasto firmamento.
Yo, ridículo y ruin, soy el paciente
esclavo. Soy el humillado eunuco.
Mi testuz sabe resistir, y llevo
sobre los pedregales la carreta
cuyas ruedas rechinan, y en cuya alta
carga de pasto crujidor, a veces
cantan versos los fuertes campesinos.
Mis ojos pensativos, al poeta,
dan sospecha de vidas misteriosas
en que reina el enigma. Me complace
meditar. Soy filósofo. Si sufro
el golpe y la punzada, reflexiono
que me concede Dios este derecho:
espantarme las moscas con el rabo.
Y sé que existe el matadero . . .

EL TORO
¡Pampa!
¡Libertad! ¡Aire y sol! Yo era el robusto
señor de la planicie, donde el aire
mi bramido llevó, cual son de un cuerno
que soplara titán de anchos pulmones.
Con el pitón a flor de piel, yo erraba
un tiempo en el gran mar de verdes hojas,
cerca del cual corría el claro arroyo
donde apagué la sed con belfo ardiente.
Luego, fui bello rey de astas agudas:
a mi voz respondían las montañas,

THE CROWD
Another bull! Another bull!

THE OX
Did you hear?
Prepare your thrust, your horns, and your hide:
your turn has come. A savage wrath,
banderillas and pikes will besiege you,
applause for the executioner; finally, death.
And above, the impassive and solitary
contemplation of the vast firmament.
I, ridiculous and despicable, am the patient
slave. I am the humiliated eunuch.
My neck knows how to endure, and I bear
over rocky ground the cart
with its squeaking wheels, where on the high
load of fodder, at times
the strong peasants sing verses.
My pensive eyes, to the poet,
arouse a suspicion of mysterious lives
where the enigma reigns. Meditating
suits me. I am a philosopher. If I suffer
a blow and a prick, I reflect
that God concedes to me this right:
to drive away flies with my tail.
And I know that the slaughterhouse exists . . .

THE BULL
Pampa!
Liberty! Sunshine and fresh air! I was the robust
master of the plains, where the air
carried my bellowing like the sound of a horn
blown by a Titan with full lungs.
With the python skin-deep, I roamed
for a time in the great sea of green blades;
nearby ran the clear stream
where I slaked my thirst with burning chops.
Then, I was a beautiful king with sharp horns:
the mountains responded to my voice,

y mi estampa, magnífica y soberbia
hiciera arder de amor a Pasifae.
Más de una vez, el huracán indómito,
que hunde los puños desgarrando el roble
bajo el cálido cielo del estío,
sopló al paso su fuego en mis narices.
Después fueron las luchas. Era el puma,
que me clavó sus garras en el flanco,
y al que enterré los cuernos en el vientre.
Y tras el día caluroso, el suave
aliento de la noche, el dulce sueño,
sentir el alba, saludar la aurora
que pone en mi testuz rosas y perlas:
ver la cuadriga de Titón que avanza
rasgando nubes con los cascos de oro,
y alrededor de la carroza lírica
desparecer las pálidas estrellas.
Hoy aguardo martirio, escarnio y muerte . . .

El Buey

¡Pobre declamador! Está a la entrada
de la vida una esfinge sonriente.
El azul es en veces negro. El astro
se oculta, desparece, muere. El hombre
es aquí el poderoso traicionero.
Para él, temor. Yo he sido en mi llanura
soberbio como tú. Sobre la grama
bramé orgulloso y respiré soberbio.
Hoy vivo mutilado, como, engordo,
la nuca inclino.

El Toro

Y bien: para ti el fresco
pasto, tranquila vida, agua en el cubo,
esperada vejez... A mí la roja
capa del diestro, reto y burla, el ronco
griterío, la arena donde clavo
la pezuña, el torero que me engaña
ágil y airoso, y en mi carne entierra

and my image, magnificent and lordly,
would make Pasiphaë burn with love.
More than once, the indomitable hurricane,
driving its fists and splitting the oak
under the hot summer sky,
blew its fire into my nostrils as it passed by.
The contests came later. It was the cougar,
sinking its claws in my flank,
and I buried my horns in its belly.
And after a sweltering day, the soft
breath of the night, sweet sleep,
sensing the dawn, greeting the sunrise
that places roses and pearls on my neck:
seeing Titan's chariot advance
as it grazes the clouds with golden hoofs,
and around the lyrical carriage
the pallid stars disappear.
Today I await martyrdom, shame, and death . . .

THE OX

Poor orator! At the entrance
of life there is a smiling sphinx.
Blue is instead black. The star
hides, disappears, dies. Man
is the treacherous one with power here.
Because of him, fear. I have been on my prairie
as lordly as you. Over the grass
I bellowed proudly and breathed without a care.
Today I live mutilated, I eat, I fatten up,
I bow my head.

THE BULL

Well then, for you fresh fodder,
a tranquil life, water in a bucket,
an expected old age . . . For me, the red
cape of a dexterous man, defiance and mockery, hoarse
shouting, the sand where I drive
my hoof, the agile and graceful toreador
who tricks me and in my flesh buries

el arpón de la alegre banderilla,
encarnizado tábano de hierro;
la tempestad en mi pulmón de bruto,
el resoplido que levanta el polvo,
mi sed de muerte en desbordado instinto,
mis músculos de bronce que la sangre
hinche en hirviente plétora de vida;
en mis ojos dos llamas iracundas,
la onda de rabia por mis nervios loca
que echa su espuma en mis candentes fauces;
el clarín del bizarro torilero
que anima la apretada muchedumbre;
el matador que enterrará hasta el pomo
en mi carne la espada; la cuadriga
de enguirnaldadas mulas que mi cuerpo
arrastrará sangriento y palpitante;
y el vítor y el aplauso a la estocada
que en pleno corazón clava el acero.
¡Oh, nada más amargo! A mí, los labios
del arma fría que me da la muerte;
tras el escarnio, el crudo sacrificio,
el horrible estertor de la agonía . . .
en tanto que el azul sagrado, inmenso,
continúa sereno, y en la altura,
el oro del gran sol rueda al poniente
en radiante apoteosis . . .

LA MUCHEDUMBRE
¡Otro toro!

EL BUEY
¡Calla! ¡Muere! Es tu tiempo.

EL TORO
¡Atroz sentencia!
Ayer el aire, el sol; hoy el verdugo . . .
¿Qué peor que este martirio?

the harpoon of his dauntless *banderilla,*
a vicious horsefly of iron;
the bestial tempest in my lung,
the panting that raises dust,
my thirst for death in a flood of instinct,
my muscles of bronze, blood-
swollen in a boiling plethora of life;
in my eyes two furious flames,
the wave of rage through my nerves, crazed,
pouring its foam into my candescent gullet;
the bugle of the dashing *torilero*
that excites the packed crowd;
the matador who will bury up to the pommel
his sword in my flesh; the team
of garlanded mules that will drag
my body bloody and throbbing;
and the cheers and applause for the thrust
of steel driven straight into my heart.
Oh, nothing more bitter! For me, the lips
of the cold weapon that kills me;
after the shame, the crude sacrifice,
the horrible death rattle . . .
while the sacred blue, immense,
continues serene, and at its height
the gold of the great sun rolls towards the west
in radiant apotheosis . . .

THE CROWD
Another bull!

THE OX
Be quiet! Die! It's your time.

THE BULL
A gruesome sentence!
Yesterday the air, the sun; today the executioner . . .
What could be worse than this martyrdom?

EL BUEY
¡La impotencia!

EL TORO
¿Y qué más negro que la muerte?

EL BUEY
¡El yugo!

THE OX

Impotence!

THE BULL

And what could be blacker than death?

THE OX

The yoke!

Early autograph of a Darío poem.

Aúm

¡Aúm! es el sol luminoso
es la inmensa pirámide, el coloso,
el corazón, el mar.
Yo sé todas las Biblias, y me llamo Takoa:
soy el padre del tigre, soy el padre del boa,
soy el todo Soar.

Reencarnaciones

Yo fui coral primero,
después hermosa piedra,
después fui de los bosques verde y colgante hiedra;
después yo fui manzana,
lirio de la campiña,
labio de niña,
una alondra cantando en la mañana;
y ahora soy un alma
que canta como canta una palma
de luz de Dios al viento.

«La tortuga de oro . . . »

A Amado Nervo

La tortuga de oro camina por la alfombra
y traza por la alfombra un misterioso estigma;
sobre su carapacho hay grabado un enigma,
y un círculo enigmático se dibuja en su sombra.

Esos signos nos dicen al Dios que no se nombra
y ponen en nosotros su autoritario estigma:
ese círculo encierra la clave del enigma
que a Minotauro mata y a la Medusa asombra . . .

246

Om

Om! is the luminous sun
is the immense pyramid, the colossus,
the heart, the sea.
I know all the Bibles, and my name is Takoa:
I am the father of the tiger, I am the father of the boa,
I am the whole Soar.

Reincarnations

I was coral first,
then beautiful stone,
then I was green ivy hanging in the woods;
then I was an apple,
a lily of the fields,
the lip of a young girl,
a skylark singing in the morning;
and now I am a soul
that sings as a palm
of God's light sings in the wind.

"The Golden Tortoise . . ."

For Amado Nervo

The golden tortoise walks across the carpet
and traces across the carpet a mysterious stigma;
on its shell there is engraved an enigma,
and an enigmatic circle is drawn in its shadow.

Those signs tell us of the God who is not named,
and put on us his authoritative stigma:
that circle encloses the key to the enigma
that slays the Minotaur and stuns the Medusa . . .

Ramo de sueños, mazo de ideas florecidas
en explosión de cantos y en floración de vidas:
sois mi pecho süave, mi pensamiento parco.

Y cuando hayan pasado las sedas de la fiesta
decidme los sutiles efluvios de la orquesta
y lo que está suspenso entre el violín y el arco . . .

PÁJAROS DE LAS ISLAS . . .

Pájaros de las islas: en vuestra concurrencia
hay una voluntad,
hay un arte secreto y una divina ciencia,
gracia de eternidad.

Vuestras evoluciones, academia expresiva,
signos sobre el azur,
riegan a Oriente ensueño, a Occidente ansia viva,
paz a Norte y a Sur.

La gloria de las rosas y el candor de los lises
a vuestros ojos son,
y a vuestras alas líricas son las brisas de Ulises,
los vientos de Jasón:

almas dulces y herméticas que al eterno problema
sois, en cifra veloz,
lo mismo que la roca, el huracán, la gema,
el iris y la voz.

Pájaros de las islas, ¡oh pájaros marinos!,
vuestros revuelos, con
ser dicha de mis ojos, son problemas divinos
de mi meditación.

Y con las alas puras de mi deseo abiertas
hacia la inmensidad,

Bouquet of dreams, a handful of ideas blooming
in an explosion of song and a flowering of lives:
you are my soft breast, my sparing thought.

And when the silks of the festival have passed,
tell me of the orchestra's subtle effluvia,
and of what is hanging between the violin and the bow . . .

BIRDS OF THE ISLANDS . . .

Birds of the islands: in your gathering
there is a resoluteness,
there is a secret art and a divine science,
a grace of eternity.

Your maneuvers, an expressive academy,
signs upon the azure,
sprinkle daydream to the Orient, vivid longing to the Occident,
peace to the North and South.

The glory of roses and the candor of lilies
are in your eyes,
and on your lyrical wings are the breezes of Ulysses,
the winds of Jason:

you sweet and hermetic souls that on the eternal problem
exist in a scribbled blur,
the same as the rock, the hurricane, the gem,
the rainbow, and the voice.

Birds of the islands: O maritime birds!
Your commotions, by
being a joy to my eyes, are divine problems
for my meditation.

And with the pure wings of my desire opened
to the immensity,

imito vuestros giros en busca de las puertas
de la única Verdad.

EN LAS CONSTELACIONES

En las constelaciones Pitágoras leía,
yo en las constelaciones pitagóricas leo;
pero se han confundido dentro del alma mía
el alma de Pitágoras con el alma de Orfeo.

Sé que soy, desde el tiempo del Paraíso, reo;
sé que he robado el fuego y robé la armonía;
que es abismo mi alma y huracán mi deseo;
que sorbo el infinito y quiero todavía . . .

Pero ¿qué voy a hacer, si estoy atado al potro
en que, ganado el premio, siempre quiero ser otro,
y en que, dos en mí mismo triunfa uno de los dos?

En la arena me enseña la tortuga de oro
hacia dónde conduce de las musas el coro
y en dónde triunfa, augusta, la voluntad de Dios.

ESPAÑOL

Yo siempre fui, por alma y por cabeza,
español de conciencia, obra y deseo,
y yo nada concibo y nada veo
sino español por mi naturaleza.

Con la España que acaba y la que empieza,
canto y auguro, profetizo y creo,
pues Hércules allí fue como Orfeo.
Ser español es timbre de nobleza.

Y español soy por la lengua divina,
por voluntad de mi sentir vibrante,

I imitate your turns in search of the doors
to the only Truth.

IN THE CONSTELLATIONS

In the constellations Pythagoras used to read,
I in the Pythagorean constellations read now;
but the soul of Pythagoras has been confused
in my soul with the soul of Orpheus.

I know that I am, since the time of Paradise, a condemned man;
I know that I have stolen fire and I stole harmony;
that my soul is an abyss and my desire a hurricane;
that I sip at infinity and still want more . . .

But what am I going to do, when I'm bound to the colt
on which, once the prize is won, I always want to be someone else,
and on which, being two in myself, only one of the two wins?

In the sand a golden tortoise shows me
where the chorus of the muses leads,
and where the august will of God triumphs.

SPANIARD

I always was, in my soul and in my head,
Spanish by conscience, works, and desire,
and I conceive nothing and I see nothing
but Spanish, by nature.

With one Spain ending and another beginning,
I sing and I bode, I prophesy and I believe,
since Hercules was like Orpheus there.
To be Spanish is a stamp of nobility.

And I am Spanish because of this divine language,
because of my vibrant determination to feel,

alma de rosa en corazón de encina;
quiero ser quien anuncia y adivina,

que viene de la pampa y la montaña:
eco de raza, aliento que culmina,
con dos pueblos que dicen: ¡Viva España!
y ¡Viva la República Argentina!

the soul of a rose in the heart of an oak;
I want to be the one who declares and divines,

who comes from the prairie and the mountain:
echo of a race, an enthusiasm that culminates
in two peoples that say: *Long live Spain!*
and *Long live the Republic of Argentina!*

Glossary

The following list is an attempt to clarify references and resolve certain questions that may arise in reading the poems in this anthology. Included are cultural, historical, literary, and mythological references that constitute a partial index of the many and complex allusions encountered in Rubén Darío; it is, no doubt, far from complete even for our limited purposes. Each entry offers quite general information that should serve as a starting point for further investigation. We cite no particular sources, and so readers should consult standard reference works if they desire more information on any subject. Readers of Spanish may wish to consult the books by A. Marasso and A. Zambrana Fonseca, cited in the "*Selected Studies on Rubén Darío*" included in this anthology.

ABELARD, Pierre (1079–1142). French theologian and philosopher whose illicit love for Héloïse became a popular literary theme. After her uncle had him castrated, Abelard became a monk and Héloïse a nun.

ACANTHUS. A prickly plant with large leaves; its representation is used to ornament the capitals of various types of architectural columns.

ACHERON. The river of woe described by Homer and Virgil; the first river encountered in the descent to the Underworld.

ACHILLES. Greek hero of the Trojan War. His mother dipped him in the Styx, a river of the Underworld, thus making him invulnerable except in the heel by which she held him.

ACTAEON. A hunter trained by the centaur Chiron. When he spied upon the goddess Diana bathing, she turned him into a stag. His own dogs tore him apart.

ADONIS. Beautiful shepherd with whom Venus fell in love. At his death, the goddess was plunged into inconsolable despair. Adonis symbolizes the omnipotence of love, which holds sway even over Venus.

254

AEGIPAN. A surname of the god Pan, though in some traditions he appears as an independent figure with his own legend. At times he is identified with the constellation Capricorn.

AEOLUS. Appointed by Zeus as keeper of the winds.

AESCULAPIUS. The Latin god of Medicine, son of the healing god Apollo.

ALEJANDRINO. A fourteen-syllable verse divided into seven-syllable hemistiches separated by a cesura. The verse was especially popular in the Middle Ages. Darío restored its use in Spanish poetry.

ALEXANDER THE GREAT (356–323 B.C.). King of Macedonia and world conquerer.

ALFONSO XIII. King of Spain from 1902 to 1931, whom Darío met in Madrid and about whom he wrote a *retrato y semblanza*, or portrait in verse.

ANACREON. Greek poet of wine and love, who lived from about 550 to 464 B.C.

ANADYOMENE. Literally *she-who-rises*, a name given to the Greek goddess Aphrodite (the Roman Venus) because of her birth from the sea.

ANAGKE. Greek word meaning destiny, fate, fatality, and necessity.

ANGELUS. A prayer in honor of the Incarnation offered morning, noon, and night with the ringing of a bell.

APHRODITE. In Greek mythology, goddess of beauty and love who corresponds to the Roman Venus.

APOLLO. Greek and Roman god of light, health, penance and purification, prophecy, music, poetry, and shepherds.

AQUILON. The north wind in Roman mythology.

ARANJUEZ. Spanish city near Madrid, site of a royal palace.

ARGENTINE SUN. Reference to the emblem of a gold sun on the flag of Argentina.

ARGONAUT. Any of fifty heroes who sailed with Jason on his quest for the golden fleece.

ARMIDA. A pagan woman in Torquato Tasso's epic poem *Gerusalemme liberata*, who wins the heart of the Christian crusader Rinaldo.

ATTIS. A shepherd so beautiful he was driven insane by the goddess Cybele when he tried to wed a mortal princess. After fleeing to the mountains, he castrated himself. Pine trees and violets are his symbols.

AURORA. The Latin name for Eos, the Greek goddess of the dawn, sister of the sun god.

BABIECA. The mighty steed of the national Spanish hero the Cid.

BACCHANTE. A priestess of Bacchus; by extension, a woman given to indulgence.

BACCHUS. Latin name for Dionysus, the Greek god of wine and fertility.

BANDERILLA. In bullfighting, a barbed dart stuck into the head and shoulders of the bull, the effect being both to enrage and weaken it. One who bears and uses *banderillas* in the fight is a *banderillero*.

BARBEY d'Aurevilly, Jules (1809-1889). French novelist who wrote about the Cid. Darío alludes to his poem "Le Cid,"written between 1872 and 1877.

BAOBAB. A tree of Africa and India.

BENGAL. A province of India.

BOLOGNA, Giovanni da (1529-1608). Sculptor and architect of Renaissance Italy, creator of a renowned bronze statue of Mercury, the Roman god. See *Mercury*.

BOREAS. The north wind in Greek mythology.

BRUNO, St. (1035-1101). Founded the Carthusian order in 1084.

CABALA. Jewish mysticism and esoteric doctrine that began to develop in Spain around 1200 A.D.

CAENEUS. Son of Hippia and Elatus, king of the Lapithae, was female at birth and named Caenis, a tradition to which Darío alludes in his "Colloquy of the Centaurs." She was later raped by Poseidon, who offered in exchange whatever she desired. The woman desired to be transformed into a man and thus became Caeneus. In addition, Poseidon made the man invulnerable. During the battle of the Lapithae and the Centaurs, the latter—unable to overcome his invulnerability—overwhelmed Caeneus and buried him under huge pine trees, from which his soul escaped in the form of a bird.

CAENIS. See *Caeneus*.

CALLIOPE. The Muse of epic poetry.

CALLISTO. A nymph from Arcadia transformed into a bear and later set among the constellations as the Big Bear or Big Dipper.

CALYX. The cup-like outer covering of a flower.

CAMPANULA. Literally *little bell* in Latin, the Mediterranean bellflower.

CANEPHOROI. Basket carriers, girls who gracefully carried baskets on their heads during solemn processions in Athens.

CANTHARIDES. Shiny green beetles known as Spanish flies, in some traditions considered an aphrodisiac.

CARDUCCI, Giosuè (1836-1913). Italian poet who turned to classical meters in reaction to the extremes of Romanticism.

CASTALIA. The spring on Mount Parnassus, consecrated to Apollo and the Muses. Its waters conferred poetic inspiration.

CELUI-QUI-NE-COMPREND-PAS. French phrase for *the one who does not understand*, and in Darío a reference to the middle class. See *Gourmont*.

CENTAURS. According to Greek mythology, a hybrid species—half man, half horse—born of Centaurus, son of Ixion and Nephele, and the mares of Thessaly. (In another version, they are the sons of Ixion and Nephele directly, and thus *Ixionids*.) Darío makes use of them in the "Colloquy of the Centaurs" to expound his ideas on various philosophical themes: life, death, the feminine element, the secret and the mystery of existence. The most illustrious centaur is Chiron, primarily for his wisdom; others of note are Pholus and Nessus. Apart from well-established mythological beings, Darío uses names rather arbitrarily, altering some and inventing others.

CERVANTES Saavedra, Miguel de (1547-1616). Spanish novelist who created the character Don Quixote.

CHARON. Old man in a black cloak who ferries the dead across the river Styx to the Underworld.

CHARTERHOUSE. Carthusian monastery. Darío refers in his poem to the Charterhouse at Valldemosa, on the island of Majorca, Spain, where the poet spent several weeks in 1906 and 1913.

CHILEAN STAR. Reference to the emblem of a star on the flag of Chile.

CHIRON. A centaur and mentor of several Greek heroes. He is traditionally the wisest of his kind and the most important in Darío's "Colloquy of the Centaurs." When he died, the gods set him among the stars as the constellation Sagittarius, the Archer.

CHOROTEGA. Indigenous people from northern Mexico who settled in the Pacific coastal zone. Darío alludes to his "Chorotega blood."

CHRYSALIS. Cocoon or formative stage of a butterfly.

CID. Arabic for *lord*, title given to Rodrigo or Ruy Díaz de Vivar (1040-1099), Spanish national hero, for his valor and prowess in campaigns against the Moors.

CLIO. The Muse of history.

CONVOLVULUS. Slender, twining, flowering plants.

CROESUS. A fabulously rich king of Lydia in the sixth century B.C.

CUADRILLA. In bullfighting, the team of men who assist the matador.

CUAUHTEMOC. Last emperor of the Aztecs (1520-1525) of Mexico, tortured by Cortés to reveal the whereabouts of hidden treasure and later hanged. Darío cites a phrase—"This is no bed of roses"—which Cuauhtemoc reputedly uttered while being tortured.

CYNEGETICS. Hunting with dogs; a traditional pose of Artemis-Diana in art.

CYPRIAN. A name for Aphrodite-Venus, referring to Cyprus and her temple there. She had a belt or sash with which she dominated men. Darío uses her as symbol of feminine power.

CYTHEREA. Another name for Aphrodite-Venus, referring to the island of Cythera where she first stepped ashore following her birth in the sea.

DEIANIRA. Wife of Hercules. The hero slew the centaur Nessus with a poison arrow when the latter attempted to rape Deianira. The dying centaur tricked her into taking his blood to use as a love potion on Hercules should she ever doubt her husband's faithfulness. She did so, and the blood proved to be a fatal poison.

DEIPHOBE. One of the Trojan heroes.

DEUCALION. After Zeus destroyed the earth with a great flood, only Deucalion and his wife Pyrrha survived, having built a wooden ark or chest to float in. After landing on Mount Parnassus, Deucalion asked the Oracle how to restore the human race and was told that he and his wife should cover their heads and toss behind them the bones of their mother, which they interpreted to be stones of Mother Earth. Deucalion's stones became men and Pyrrha's became women.

DIANA. The Latin name for Artemis, virgin goddess of the hunt and moonlight and protector of the young.

DÍAZ MIRÓN, Salvador (1853-1928). Mexican poet and playwright, author of *Poesías* (1886) and *Lascas* (1901).

DIOSCOURI. Castor and Pollux, brothers of Helen of Troy and the sons of Zeus and Leda, whom the god seduced in the form of a swan. Both became Argonauts.

DODECASYLLABLE. A twelve-syllable verse, sometimes equally divided into hemistiches like the *alejandrino*, and sometimes divided into five- and seven-syllable units, the rhythm of several traditional and popular poetic forms. As with the *alejandrino*, Darío revived its use in Spanish-language poetry.

EBURNEAN. Made of ivory.

EGO SUM LUX ET VERITAS ET VITA. Latin for *I am light and truth and life*; conflation of two sayings of Christ Jesus.

EHEU. Latin interjection that is the first word of Horace's famous ode "Eheu, fugaces . . . , " meaning *alas, oh dear, oh no*, etc. As does the Roman poet, Darío bemoans the brevity of life.

ELAGABALUS. Roman emperor (218-22), whose life is always associated with lavishness, madness, cruelty, and licentiousness. Darío's interest lies mainly in the fabled luxury of the emperor's court.

ENDYMION. A beautiful shepherd to whom Zeus gave eternal youth in the form of never-ending slumber. His lover, the moon-goddess Selene, comes out each night to visit him.

EPHEBE. A boy between sixteen and twenty years old, the period which marked his coming of age in ancient Athens.

ERATO. The Muse of erotic poetry.

EROS. The Greek god of love, equivalent to the Roman Cupid.

EROS, VITA, LUMEN. Latin for *Love, Life, Light.*

EUROPA. Daughter of the Phoenician king, she was carried off to Crete by Zeus in the shape of a bull.

EUTERPE. The Muse of lyric poetry and song. She is represented with a single or double flute, instrument of the Dionysian cult.

FAUN. A rural deity resembling the satyr.

FLORA. Roman goddess of the springtime and of flowers.

GAITA. Musical wind instrument resembling the bagpipe. In poetry, the *gaita gallega* indicates a form of hendecasyllable.

GALATEA. A sea nymph in love with the shepherd Acis, she is pursued by the monstrous cyclops Polyphemus, who crushes Acis with a rock. The Spanish poet Luis de Góngora wrote a famous Baroque poem on the theme, *La fábula de Polifemo y Galatea*, with which Darío was familiar. See *Góngora.*

GARCILASO de la Vega (1500-1536). One of the most famous lyrical poets in Spanish, who revolutionized poetry by mastering and popularizing Italian versification and poetic forms like the sonnet.

GAVOTTE. A fast and lively French dance of the seventeenth century that was popular all over Europe.

GOLCONDA. City in India famous for diamonds and other treasures. It was the capital of a vast empire until 1687.

GÓNGORA y Argote, Luis de (1561-1627). One of the great poets of Spain's Golden Age, known for an exquisite style, at times difficult and erudite, called *gongorismo* after the poet.

GOURMONT, Remy de (1858-1915). French novelist, playwright, and critic, whom Darío read and about whom he wrote an article. One of Gourmont's characters of great interest to Darío was a certain Mr. *"Celui-qui-ne-comprend-pas,"* symbol of the *bourgeoisie* or middle class.

GRACES. In Greek mythology, the three goddesses of charm and beauty: Thalia (blossom), Aglaïa (brilliance), and Euphrosyne (joy).

GRACIÁN, Baltasar (1601-1658). Prose writer of the Spanish Golden Age, master of the cultured *conceptista* style and author of *El criticón*, an allegorical novel.

GRANT, Ulysses (1822-1885). U.S. general and president from 1869 to 1877. There is no record of the conversation between Grant and Hugo to which Rubén Darío alludes in the poem "To Roosevelt." However, Grant did visit Paris in 1877, and Hugo attacked him in a number of writings.

GROUSSAC, Paul (1848-1929). French-Argentine writer and feared literary critic.

HARMONY. Daughter of Ares and Aphrodite. Roman mythology converted her into the personification of order. Darío imagines music as the fairy Harmony in her rhythmic flight.

HECATE. Greek goddess of night, the underworld, and the moon. Dogs were consecrated to and associated with her.

HÉLOÏSE. See *Abelard*.

HENDECASYLLABLE. One of the principal verse forms in Spanish poetry since the Renaissance, when it was popularized by Garcilaso de la Vega; a verse of eleven syllables customarily accentuated on the sixth and tenth syllables or on the fourth, eighth, and tenth syllables.

HERACLES. The greatest of Greek heroes, son of Zeus and a mortal woman. Traditionally armed with a club—sometimes with bow and arrow—and wearing a lion skin, he is generally held to be the strongest man in mythology.

HERCULES. The Roman name for Heracles.

HERODIAS. Wife of Herod and mother of Salome, with whom she schemed to behead John the Baptist. The women symbolize vengeance and cruelty.

HESIOD. After Homer, the earliest Greek epic poet whose name has survived; his *Theogony* relates the history of the gods and creation.

HEXAMETER. Verse composed of six metric feet, the first five of which are often dactyls and the sixth metric foot a trochee, with a cesura falling between the third and fourth metric foot; the modern hexameter is based on the characteristic rhythm of Greek and Latin narrative and didactic poetry.

HILARION, St. (291-371). Disciple of St. Anthony and founder of monastic life in Palestine. Having sold all his possessions, he retreated into the wilderness.

HIPPODAMIA. At her wedding to Pirithous, one of the guests—the centaur Eurytion—attempted to steal the bride, causing the legendary battle between the centaurs and the Lapithae.

HOLMES, Augusta (1848-1903). French composer of Irish origin and admirer of Richard Wagner.

HORACE (65-8 B.C.). Roman poet famous for satires and odes.

HORMUZ. Island in the Persian Gulf celebrated for its pearls.

HOURS. The four goddesses of the seasons and of natural order.

HUGO, Victor (1802-1885). French novelist, poet, and playwright, for whom Darío felt great admiration.

HYBLAEAN. Reference to the ancient Sicilian city of Hybla, famous for the honey produced in the area.

HYMENEAL. A wedding song, from Hymen, the Greek god of marriage.

HYMETTUS. Mountain ridge of central Greece, famous for its honey and its shrines.

HYPERESTHESIA. Abnormal sensitivity.

HYPERION. Father of the sun, the moon, and dawn—that is, the gods Helios, Selene, and Eos. In Homer, synonymous with Helios, the Greek god of the sun.

HYPSIPYLE. Leader of the women of Lemnos, who killed all the men on the island, except the old king. At times Rubén Darío uses the name for *butterfly*, following a classification of the Danish entomologist Fabricius (*Genera Insectorum*, 1776).

INCA. One of the kings of the Quechua peoples of the Peruvian Andes, whose empire fell to the Spanish in the early sixteenth century.

IONIAN or IONIC. Of an ancient people and their culture in eastern Greece and Ionia; also a reference to Ion of Chios, lyrical poet and historian of the fifth century B.C.

IRIS. Goddess of the rainbow that joins heaven and earth.

ITE, MISSA EST. Latin for *Go, the mass is over*, a phrase that preceded the final benediction of the Roman Catholic mass.

IXION. King of the Lapithae and father of the centaurs through the cloud goddess Nephele.

IXIONID. Son of Ixion, which is to say, a centaur.

JIMÉNEZ, Juan Ramón (1881-1958). Spanish poet and winner of the Nobel Prize, who was also a friend, supporter, and editor of Rubén Darío.

JOVE. Variation of the chief Roman god Jupiter.

JUPITER. Analogous to the Greek Zeus, the chief Roman god in heaven, and for this reason in charge of weather. Whether as Jupiter or as Zeus, in a number of myths he transforms himself—into bull, swan, golden shower—in order to seduce a mortal woman.

KING LOUIS XIV (1638-1715). The Sun King of France.

LAMPADARY. One who carries a lighted taper in a religious procession.

LEDA. A woman seduced by Zeus-Jupiter in the shape of a swan. Two eggs were produced by this union: from one egg emerged Helen and from the other Castor and Pollux, the Dioscouri. Leda symbolizes the erotic in Darío.

LEMURES. To the Romans, ghosts in fearsome shapes wandering through the night.

LONGFELLOW, Henry Wadsworth (1807-1882). U.S. poet who wrote *Evangeline* in dactylic hexameter.

LOPE DE VEGA y Carpio (1562-1635). One of the great dramatists and poets of the Golden Age of Spain.

LUTETIA. Roman name for the city of Paris.

LYMPH. A spring of clear water.

MACHADO, Antonio (1875-1939). Spanish lyrical poet, author of *Soledades* (1903) and *Campos de Castilla* (1912).

MADRID CÓMICO. Spanish literary magazine famous for parodies, satire, and humor about cultural life in Spain in the early twentieth century.

MADRIGAL. A song for several unaccompanied voices that was popular from the fifteenth to the seventeenth centuries; also a short lyrical poem.

MAMMON. The Phoenician god of wealth and greed.

MANES. To the Romans, divine spirits of the dead that visit this world at certain seasons.

MELPOMENE. The Muse of tragedy.

MEMENTO, HOMO . . . From the Latin phrase used by Roman Catholic priests on Ash Wednesday. *Memento, homo, quia pulvis es et in pulverem reverteris:* Remember, man, you are dust and to dust you will return.

MERCURY. Roman god identified with the Greek Hermes, messenger of the gods, protector of fertility and crops, and inventor of the lyre. As in the famous statue by Giovanni da Bologna, the god is often portrayed naked with wings on his feet and helmet, and carrying the caduceus, or herald's staff.

METEMPSYCHOSIS. Transmigration of souls after death, into human or animal form.

MINERVA. Roman goddess identified with the Greek Athena, born from the forehead of Zeus-Jupiter in full armor, and goddess of wisdom and virginity.

MISERERE. Latin word with which Psalm 51 begins: *Have mercy . . .*

MODERNISMO. Hispanic movement in art and literature at the end of the nineteenth century and beginning of the twentieth, which found its first full-blown representation in Rubén Darío. In Darío *modernismo* may be divided into two aspects: (1) the *aesthetic*, typified by the cultivation of the word and the metaphor, renovation, artistic freedom, exoticism, classicism, cosmopolitanism, symbolism, and irrationalism; and (2) the *existential*, centering on the poet as hero or sacred bard, anguish, eroticism, the problem of

God, rebellion, and elitism. *Modernismo* should not be confused either with the *modernismo brasileiro* during the 1920s in Brazil or with the Modernist movement of English-language writers, who may share some concerns and impulses with the Hispanic *modernistas*, but neither origin nor acquaintance.

MONTEZUMA (1466-1520). Aztec emperor at the time of the Spanish arrival in Mexico, he died in the early skirmishes after being taken prisoner by Cortés and was succeeded by Cuauhtemoc. His name is also spelled *Moctezuma*.

MORTUI ESTIS. Latin for *You all are dead.*

MUSES. Nine goddesses of arts and sciences who dwell on Olympus and inspire human beings: *Calliope*, goddess of the epic; *Clio*, goddess of history; *Erato*, goddess of love poetry; *Euterpe*, goddess of lyric poetry; *Melpomene*, goddess of tragedy; *Polyhymnia*, goddess of sacred song; *Terpsichore*, goddess of the dance; *Thalia*, goddess of comedy; and *Urania*, goddess of astronomy. Apollo was their protector.

MULETA. In bullfighting, the matador's baton from which a red cape hangs.

NABOB. Originally a native ruler in India, now used to describe the very wealthy.

NAGRANDAN. Relating to an indigenous tribe of Central America. Darío alludes to his "Nagrandan blood."

NAIAD. Nymphs of rivers and streams.

NARCISSUS. A beautiful youth condemned by the gods to fall in love with his own reflection in the water, for which he pined away and died; or, alternatively, he drowned in an attempt to embrace his reflection.

NAXOS. Greek island where Theseus abandoned Ariadne, a place famous for its wine, its marble, and its diverse agriculture.

NEBUCHADNEZZAR. Greatest of the Babylonian kings mentioned in the Bible.

NELUMBO. Indian water lilies with blue-green leaves and white or dark red flowers.

NEPHELIBATA. Greek neologism for *Cloud-walker*. Darío alludes to the dreamer who walks on the clouds.

NESSUS. Centaur who served as ferryman when Hercules and his new wife Deianira came to cross the river. As he carried Deianira on his back, he made a sexual pass, whereupon she cried to her husband, who shot Nessus with an arrow. The dying centaur tricked Deianira into using his blood as a love charm on the wayward Hercules; the blood proved to be instead a fatal poison.

NETZAHUALCOYOTL. Aztec warrior and poet, sovereign of Texcoco until 1472, the year of his death.

NIMROD. Called in the Bible "the mighty hunter before the Lord" and the first king of Babel. He is used as a symbol of tyranny.

OCEAN. The great river surrounding the world, the beginning and boundary of all things.

ODOR DI FEMINA. Italian for the *scent of a woman*.

OMAR KHAYYÁM. Persian poet of the twelfth century, author of *The Rubáiyát*.

OMPHALE. Queen of Lydia, for whom Hercules—dressed as a woman—was forced to spin and weave. Captivated by the hero's valor, she freed and then married him. Darío uses her as a symbol of feminine power over the male.

ORACLE. A place where gods prophesy through a chosen priest or priestess, the most famous being the oracle at Delphi.

ORLANDO. Hero of a number of epics, including Ariosto's *Orlando furioso*; he corresponds to the French hero Roland.

ORMAZD. Supreme being of Zoroastrianism in ancient Persia.

ORPHEUS. Mythical poet and one of the Argonauts, whose lyrical power could tame wild animals and move rocks and trees. His lyre was made of tortoiseshell.

OVID Naso, Publius (43 B.C.-17 A.D.). Roman poet, author of *Ars Amandi* [*The Art of Love*] and *Metamorphoses* [*Transformations*].

PALENQUE. Mayan city of great splendor in pre-Columbian Mexico.

PALLIUM. Roman name for a large cloak typically worn by philosophers.

PAN. Greek god of the woods and hills, connected to satyrs and Dionysus or Bacchus, who typically has goat legs and carries the syrinx or shepherd's pipe. The Romans identified him as Faunus. He is one of the most frequently mentioned gods in Darío's poems.

PANDEAN. One devoted to the cult of Pan.

PANDORA. Woman created out of clay whose curiosity brought all manner of woes into the world when she opened a box which she was forbidden to open. The last to escape the box, and quite different from the rest, was Hope.

PANIC. Of or related to the god Pan.

PASIPHAË. Queen of Crete. Poseidon caused her to fall in love with a white bull, with whom she had a son, the Minotaur, half-man and half-bull.

PAVAN. From the Spanish for *peacock*, a slow stately dance for couples.

PEGASUS. The winged horse of Greek mythology, associated with Eos-Aurora (Dawn) and the Muses.

PEPLUS. A long garment, hanging in folds, worn by women in ancient Greece.

PHOEBUS. Name given to Apollo, the god of light.

PHIDIAS. Greek sculptor of the fifth century B.C., creator of the statue of Athena in the Parthenon.

PHILOMELA. In Greek myth, the sister of Procne; she was turned into a nightingale. The name frequently appears in Darío as a poetic word for *nightingale.*

PHOCAS. "To Phocas the Peasant" refers to the poet's son Rubén Darío Sánchez, his first child with Francisca. The boy died when he was just two years old. The name and the expression come from "Phocas le Jardinier" (1898), by the French poet Vielé-Griffin.

PHOLUS. Hospitable centaur who offered Hercules wine from the god Dionysus, thus provoking a riot among his kind. Ironically, Pholus was killed by one of the arrows shot by Hercules in the brawl.

PHRYNE. A courtesan of great beauty and influence in ancient Athens who served as the model for a statue of Aphrodite by Praxiteles in the fourth century B.C. In his "Autumn Poem" Darío has Phryne model for Phidias, an illustrious Greek sculptor of an earlier century.

PICADOR. In bullfighting, one who jabs at the bull from horseback.

PIERIDES. Another name for the Muses; from Pieria, their birthplace in Thessaly.

POLYHYMNIA. The Muse of sacred songs.

POMPADOUR, Marquise de. Jeanne Antoinette Poisson (1721-1764), mistress of King Louis XV of France.

POMPANO. Food fish with spiny fins and a forked tail.

PROMETHEUS. Titan who stole fire from Olympus for men's use, which led the gods to create Pandora, the first woman, to punish them.

PROPYLAEUM. A porch or vestibule leading into a temple enclosure.

PSYCHE. In Greek mythology, a beautiful woman with butterfly wings who personifies the human soul and is the beloved of Eros-Cupid.

PYRRHA. See *Deucalion.*

PYTHAGORAS. Greek philosopher, mathematician, and mystic of the sixth century B.C., whose doctrine included the transmigration of souls and the harmony of the universe based on number and mathematical principles, the music of the spheres.

QUEVEDO y Villegas, Francisco de (1580-1645). One of the great poets of the Golden Age of Spain, justly famous for his profound use of language and conceits, as well as for biting satires.

QUINTANA, Manuel José (1772-1857). Patriotic Spanish poet whose literary impulses fall between the Enlightenment and Romanticism.

REQUIESCAT IN PACE. Latin for *Rest in peace.*

RODRIGO DÍAZ DE VIVAR. See the *Cid.*

ROMANCE. Traditional Spanish ballad verse form, consisting of eight-syllable lines; only even-numbered verses are rhymed in assonance, and therefore the poem nearly always ends on an even-numbered line.

ROOSEVELT, Theodore (1858-1919). U.S. president whose Roosevelt Doctrine claimed the right of the United States to interfere in the affairs of all nations in the Western Hemisphere. After the Spanish-American War of 1898, in which he served with his "Rough Riders" in Cuba, Roosevelt's statements—"Walk softly and carry a big stick," for example—and his policies were considered by many Hispanics as provocative and imperialist.

SALOME. See *Herodias.*

SATURN. Roman god of crops identified with the Greek god Cronos, who routinely devoured his own children as soon as they were born; expelled by his son Jupiter, he brought agriculture to the Latin people. His Greek name being easily confused with that of Chronos (Time), Saturn came to be regarded as the god of time.

SATYR. In Greek mythology, libertine spirits of the mountains and woods who have pointed ears and a short tail, gambol with nymphs, and carouse with Dionysus. They symbolize lust and debauchery, and Darío frequently identifies with them.

SATYRESS. A female version of the satyr, especially in terms of sexual appetite, used by Darío.

SCOPAS. Renowned Greek sculptor of the fourth century B.C.

SEPTENTRIONAL. Referring to the north or the northern regions. In Darío, it may refer to "northern" peoples: the U.S. or the Anglo-Saxon cultures.

SERVENTESIO. Stanza form consisting of four (usually eleven-syllable) verses that rhyme ABAB.

SILVA. Poetic form consisting traditionally of seven- and eleven-syllable verses that rhyme in consonance according to no fixed scheme.

SILVA ARROMANZADA. Poetic form consisting of seven- and eleven-syllable verses that rhyme in assonance only in even-numbered verses (like the *romance*) and are sometimes divided into four-verse stanzas.

SILVANUS. Roman god identified with Faunus, and sometimes with Pan; protector of woods, fields, and gardens.

SIRENUSAE. Three rocky islands inhabited by the mythological sirens, mermaids whose irresistible song lured passing sailors to their doom.

SISTRUM. A metal rattle used in the worship of Isis.

SPANISH LION. Reference to the emblem of a lion on the Spanish flag.

SPES. Latin for *hope*.

STACCATI. Italian term used in music to indicate a series of abrupt, detached elements.

SUM. Latin for *I am*.

SYLVAN. Spirits or sprites of the woods associated with the Roman god Silvanus.

SYRINX. Pan's pipe, consisting of seven to nine reeds, used by shepherds.

TERMINUS. Roman god of boundaries, protector of the stone markers driven into the earth at boundary lines.

TERPSICHORE. The Muse of dancing.

THALIA. The Muse of comedy.

THERESA, St (1515-1582). Spanish nun who wrote about her mystical unions with God.

THYRSIS. Shepherd in Virgil's *Eclogues*. The eighteenth-century European courts frequently revived bucolic themes from earlier times, and thus the appearance of Thyrsis, Amaryllis, etc., was widespread in literature and painting: shepherds and shepherdesses representing a lost Golden Age, to which Darío refers in the scene at Versailles.

TITAN. Any of the giant, powerful deities overthrown by the Olympian gods after a terrible war for supremacy; the name is also used for their descendants, such as Prometheus and the sun god Helios.

TITIAN (1477-1576). Venetian painter.

TIZONA. One of the Cid's legendary swords.

TOLSTOY, Leo (1828-1910). Russian writer, author of *War and Peace* and other novels. Darío mentions him in "To Roosevelt" for his austere and humble life.

TORILERO. In bullfighting, the one in charge of the bullpen (the *toril*).

TRITON. Mythical being in the shape of a man from the waist up and a dolphin below, and who blows on a seashell to control the waves.

URANIA. The Muse of astronomy.

VALLE-INCLÁN, Ramón del (1866-1936). Spanish poet, novelist, and playwright, author of *Sonata de otoño* and *Divinas palabras*.

VARONA, Enrique José (1849-1933). Cuban patriot in that island's struggle for independence from Spain.

VEGA BELGRANO, Carlos (1858-1930). Argentine writer and journalist, editor of the daily *El Tiempo* and friend of Rubén Darío.

VENUS. See *Aphrodite*.

VENUS DE MILO. Famous statue of Venus in which the goddess is missing both arms.

VERLAINE, Paul (1844-1896). French symbolist poet. One of the writers—Victor Hugo being the other—whom Darío most admired.

VESTAL. One of the virgin priestesses of the Roman goddess Vesta.

WALES, Prince of. Darío refers perhaps to the man who would become Edward VII, King of Great Britain and Ireland (1901-1910).

WHITMAN, Walt (1819-1892). U.S. poet, author of *Leaves of Grass*.

XIMENA. Wife of the Cid, who figures prominently in works about him.

ZEPHYR. Personification of the mild west wind, associated with springtime.